Kindergarten
in Photographs

A Mentor Teacher Shares Effective Organizing Strategies and Management Tips
to Help You Create a Dynamic Teaching and Learning Environment

JASMINE GREENE

■SCHOLASTIC

NEW YORK • TORONTO • LONDON • AUCKLAND • SYDNEY
MEXICO CITY • NEW DELHI • HONG KONG • BUENOS AIRES

Dedication

Dad, Mom, John, Ivy, and Nolan

Boo, Oliver, Magoo, Romeo, Maxwell, Willy,
Casey Jean, Charles, Mo, Missy, Pippy, and Cinder

You are the love in my life.
My past, my present, and my future.

Acknowledgments

Thank you to my dear friend and editor, Mela Ottaiano
for your friendship and support.
Thanks to Maria Lilja for your creative design,
layout, and attention to detail.

Many thanks to my friends and colleagues who have shared
their ideas, time, and resources with me over the years:
Judy Mandel, Irene Delgado, Janet Connelly, Cathy Finch, Margie Heft,
Karen Ritchey, Marianne Silva-Flores, Molly Stewart, Jeremy Robles,
Karol Singer, Mary Jean Altman, Lynn Greer, and Sue Sweet.

Editor: Mela Ottaiano
Cover and interior design: Maria Lilja
Photos: Jasmine Greene, Aiko Andrews, Shari Osuch, and Amber Johnson

ISBN-13: 978-0-545-23138-1 • ISBN-10: 0-545-23138-8

Contents

Introduction

Kindergarten is a milestone for students and their parents. Students wave good-bye at the door and walk into a new world where they are expected to become independent thinkers and lifelong learners, and make good decisions about how to manage themselves. It is my goal to provide students with a supportive, loving, and engaging environment so they can become successful students and develop that essential lifelong love for learning.

Through hands-on experiences, students gain confidence in their own abilities and develop a sense of accomplishment and independence. Creating a joyful learning environment fosters curiosity and opens up students to taking risks in their learning. Because the human brain is a pattern-seeking, meaning-making, purpose-detecting organ, in the classroom I strive to maintain routines and consistency, provide positive feedback, and teach explicitly in order to support student engagement.

Managing a kindergarten classroom with more than 20 four- and five-year-olds is a formidable task for any teacher. First of all, kindergarten poses a unique challenge as students (and often parents) are taking their first big leap into the unknown and are unsure of what will be expected of them. You can ease this

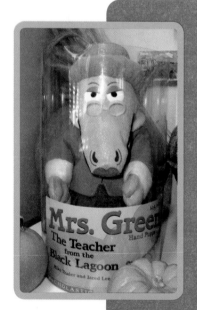

BASIC KEYS TO KINDERGARTEN

My approach to teaching kindergarten follows the keys below. In my experience, they enable all children to become successful students. When they are in place students learn, teachers are proud, and parents are happy.

- Learning is a joyful experience.

- Students feel their classroom is a loving, safe environment.

- Learning is hands-on and meaningful for students.

- Focus is on individual growth and development.

- Students practice in order to improve in any subject area.

- Students are expected to do their best.

- Students are responsible for their words and actions.

- Teachers and parents maintain high expectations for all students.

- Teachers and parents guide students to make good choices.

- Open communication exists between parents and teachers throughout the year.

- The classroom is a community of learners where students, parents, and teachers support one another and celebrate success.

MAKE EVERY DAY COUNT! The sign above our math calendar captures the spirit of our classroom. Throughout the year, I share with students that our learning time is precious and we have to make every moment count. I want them to have a sense of urgency and understand that there is no time to waste because we have lots to learn in kindergarten.

transition to school by having your own clearly defined set of rules, procedures, and expectations. The time you initially spend to think about and set up structures and procedures will pay off tremendously when you see that your students know what to do.

Organization is crucial to successfully utilizing learning time. When everything has a place, students are able to become independent and responsible parties in maintaining the classroom environment. Since kindergarten requires frequent transitions and lots of hands-on materials, your year will include a constant stream of getting out materials to use. To maintain order in your classroom, putting them away in a timely fashion is a must. When you are organized you will be in control and efficiently able to manage your busy kindergarten day.

Take advantage of the fact that kindergarteners are primed to learn independence. If you clearly and consistently teach them your expectations at the beginning of the year, they will respond and soon the magic will appear. You can count on them to help you run the show. When parents and students learn your routines, school is a joyous place to be.

CHAPTER 1

Beginning the Year Smoothly

There are so many things to do before the year even starts. I have found the more prepared I am, the better my year begins. All kindergarten teachers know that the first weeks of school, as students are getting adjusted to their new routines, are the toughest. One of the most important things is to be mentally prepared. You need to be ready to tell students what the rules and procedures are for your classroom, which means you must first be clear about these yourself. How will students ask to go to the restroom without interrupting learning? What will they do when their pencil breaks? Can they get drinks anytime they want to? There are myriad scenarios that you need to think through before your year begins.

Beginning the year with a checklist (such as the one on page 26) helps ensure you don't forget anything and are not caught off guard.

The following sections describe the areas where I have focused most of my preparation efforts to help ease the transition to the new school year.

Defining Rules

"Slow and steady" is my motto as I teach children the rules that lay the foundation for behavior expectations throughout the year. I like rules that are measurable and objective. I begin teaching them using a class book, which I made with photographs of students following each rule. After reading the book, I select students to role-model each rule for their peers. Role-modeling is a very positive and effective technique. Here are some other techniques that work well:

- Have students repeat back rules, which reinforces learning. Students also explain why the rules are necessary.

- Provide very specific praise to a student who's in close proximity to someone who is being disruptive. This shows students who aren't following the rules the type of behavior you are looking for.

- Give disruptive students private reprimands in a brief, clear, neutral tone immediately.

Kindergarteners thrive on positive reinforcement and will make great strides with it. Give attention to what you want to see happen. Positive attention and feedback creates a friendly atmosphere in the classroom and encourages young

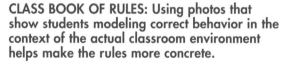

CLASS BOOK OF RULES: Using photos that show students modeling correct behavior in the context of the actual classroom environment helps make the rules more concrete.

RULES IN A POCKET CHART: The rules are kept on sentence strips in our rolling pocket chart where we can review them as infractions occur in the beginning of the year. Eventually, as students begin to memorize them, they are posted on the wall near the front of the room, creating space in the pocket chart for new learning activities.

TEACHER TALK: I often remind students of how their parents might view their behavior:

66 Your parents will be so proud of how you are able to keep your hands to yourself at school. I am going to be sure to tell them about your excellent self-control today. 99

children to do their best. I verbalize the positive behavior I want to see throughout the year so students hear continual positive feedback about what they are doing well. Establishing a predictable environment and providing immediate feedback to students helps eliminate negative behavior.

I also create a chart in the beginning of the year with four quadrants and these headings: Rug Rules, How to Listen, Classroom Rules, and How to Work at Centers (see page 8). During our first week of school, we write this chart together. I guide students and then reword their suggestions to ensure we get the main ideas and explicit behavior expectations on our chart. Utilizing our chart pad allows me to have priority access to the rules during the first month of school. Reviewing the chart or a portion of it is a ritual before beginning our activities. I always remind myself to establish class rules in a slow, steady manner. It is tempting to jump too quickly into curriculum, but in doing so you may lose time throughout the year attending to behavior issues. I find that when I am clear about behavior expectations before my lesson, I have fewer interruptions. The process requires patience.

Beginning the Year Smoothly

Students need time to absorb all the new information they receive in the beginning of the year. We review our classroom rules, rug rules, directions for listening, and how to work at centers every day during the first month of school.

Rug Rules	How to Listen
1. Come quietly, ready to learn	1. One speaker at a time
2. Sit criss cross, hug fingers	2. Eyes on the speaker
3. Listen and learn	3. Think about the message
4. Share your ideas	
Classroom Rules	**How to Work at Centers**
1. Follow directions - 1st time	1. Whisper
2. Use quiet voices	2. Be polite
3. Raise your hand	3. Share
4. Keep hands to yourself	4. Stay focused
5. Use kind words and actions	5. Do your best

TEACHER TALK: I look for opportunities to show students with behavior problems a new picture of themselves:

❝I like how you raised your hand instead of calling out. That is showing respect to your friends.❞

As the teacher, you will need to teach expectations for routine procedures in order to have a productive year. Since kindergarteners need repetition and consistency in order to learn, this chart becomes my teaching aid for creating these conditions.

TEACHER TALK: I make students aware of how their actions affect others:

❝You made your friend happy when you invited her to make chalk pictures with you at recess. That is a good way to make a friend.❞ Or, ❝You hurt Brian's feelings when you wouldn't share your red crayon with him. In our class we share everything.❞

Nice things to say

I like your painting. *Warm fuzzy*

Are you alright?

Do you want to play with me?

I am sorry.

Excuse me, you're in my spot.

May I have it when you're done?

It's nice to meet you.

May I have help please?

After reading *The Original Warm Fuzzy Tale*, students and I develop a chart of nice things to say. Students are acknowledged for using Warm Fuzzies with peers and teachers at school throughout the year.

WARM FUZZIES AND COLD PRICKLIES In *The Original Warm Fuzzy Tale* written by Claude Steiner, Warm Fuzzy and Cold Prickly are describing words for inanimate objects the characters give away in the story. Warm Fuzzies are kind words and actions which make people feel good. Cold Pricklies, unkind words and actions that make people feel bad, are the polar opposite. Young children can really relate to these concepts, which help them gain an understanding about making good choices. We use the terms Warm Fuzzy and Cold Prickly throughout the year to describe students' actions. Mostly we have lots of Warm Fuzzies, which makes everyone feel good.

Establishing Procedures and Routines

Here are some ideas for establishing procedures to address the day-to-day routines of a typical kindergarten classroom.

BACKPACKS & LUNCHBOXES

Students keep all their belongings together in their backpacks and have access to them at recess, lunch, and the end of the day. They learn that "packing up" means putting their belongings inside their backpack, not on, under, or next to it. I teach students the words *inside* and *outside* through a mini-lesson using their bodies. Packing up independently is something that takes time to learn. Most young students are still learning how to manage their belongings.

LUNCH MONEY

In my class, I highly encourage parents to pre-pay for their child's lunch and to manage their cafeteria accounts through the school office, the cafeteria, or online. If they choose to send money on a daily basis, I make it clear that I do not handle money. Students are responsible for it. As a new teacher, I used to take money in the morning and keep it in an envelope with each student's number on it. I found that it took up too much of my time and distracted me during our morning time. With my new policy, parents and students are accountable and my morning is less hectic.

BACKPACKS OUTSIDE ON BENCH: When possible, store backpacks away from where students are spending their learning time. This minimizes a potential source of distraction.

LUNCH SURVEY: In the morning on the first day of school, parents fill out a lunch survey so I have the information I need to help the students with their first experience in the school cafeteria. This helps me know who to remind to get their lunch boxes and who to direct to the hot lunch line in the cafeteria.

Student mailboxes

United States Post Office
Ocean Beach Station

Mrs. Green
The Teacher
from the
Black Lagoon

TABLE WITH BASKET NEXT TO MAILBOXES: Having one place for the variety of paperwork coming and going each day helps me keep track of it all.

MAIL CENTER Our mail center is located next to the front door for easy access in packing up. The area contains the students' mailboxes and a big basket that holds notes, book orders, and home projects I need to give individual parents.

On top of the mailboxes I keep a tray that holds flyers or notes from school to be sorted. Volunteers file these items in students' communication folders (see page 81) throughout the week.

Students are taught to manage their own mailbox. In the beginning of the year after students are assigned a class number, I teach them how to file their class work in their mailboxes.

Students also have some responsibility managing the basket, since it's also a depository for notes that they carry in from parents in the morning. Students know if they have a book order, a note from home, or any other paperwork for me they must deposit it in the basket on their way into the classroom. This keeps my hands free in the morning. I check the basket during recess and file any paperwork I receive. I also put my own notes in the basket to give to parents at the end of the day.

LINING UP AND WALKING IN LINE

There is a designated spot where students line up when we enter the classroom. When we leave the classroom there is a different spot. These spots help students understand where our line begins when entering or leaving the room. While walking in line we use three simple rules: Eyes forward, ducktails (hands behind our backs), and stay together. In the beginning of the year we always review the rules before lining up, and I praise students who follow them while we practice walking around our track. I always use stopping points when we walk long distances to ensure the group stays together. I also teach a quiet signal, which looks like an animal listening: Middle and ring fingers touch the thumb, and the pinkie and pointer fingers go up in the air like ears. I use this signal anytime before entering a "Quiet Zone." This signifies that our mouths are closed and our ears are open. Before we pass by other classrooms or enter the library, I remind students that we are showing respect for other students' learning by passing by quietly. If students do not come in quietly, we go back outside and repeat the process. They quickly learn that they are expected to come in quietly so that learning can begin immediately.

Quiet signal

Rules for Walking in Line

1. Eyes forward

2. Ducktails

hands crossed behind your back

3. Stay together

TEACHER TALK: There are two chants we use before coming into our classroom. The first one was taught to me by my colleague:

66 Hands up high, hands down low, behind our backs, and away we go. 99

The second one is a question I ask, 66 How do we come to the rug? 99 Students chant back, 66 Quietly, ready to learn, 99 and then we proceed to walk in.

Students practicing walking on the first day of school.

WALKING ROUTES Open, clear pathways are a must in the classroom. I teach students specific walking routes to the rug and for leaving the rug to go out the door. This keeps students from scattering throughout the room when I dismiss them.

COMING TO THE RUG Before entering the classroom, I routinely ask the class: "How do we come to the rug?" Students respond, "Quietly, ready to learn." Students stay in line and walk in quietly. This is a ritual we repeat throughout the year. Individuals who do not use self-control are asked to go back and try again. If there are many offenders, the whole class repeats the action in order to show that it is the expectation every time.

Students are taught to come to the rug in an orderly manner when entering the room or finishing an activity at a center or their seat.

HOW TO SIT ON THE RUG The expectation is that students sit in their assigned spots when we are in rows and that they make a choice of where to sit when we sit in a circle. The rows help me with structure when I need it in the morning during our literacy block. Students hear, "Keep your eyes on the learning" and are encouraged to share their ideas during rug time.

HOW TO LISTEN I share these simple rules with students: One speaker at a time, eyes on the speaker, and think about the message. Another one of our classroom rules is to raise your hand to speak.

TEACHER TALK: On the rug I use proximity praise to help remind students how to sit.

"Cian, all your friends can see because you are sitting crisscross applesauce. Thank you Emily for hugging your fingers." I also give gentle reminders to specific students by saying, "Check yourself."

TEACHER TALK: Give students a purpose for listening,

"I want you to listen for…"

Use open-ended questions that begin with *who, what, where, when,* and *why.*

Students sit "crisscross applesauce" with hands in their laps. If students follow these specific rules, there are very few incidents of neighbors bumping or bothering each other and therefore there is a greater focus on learning.

How To Listen
1. Stop talking. [stop]
2. Turn your shoulders TO face the speaker.
3. Look in the speakers eyes.
4. Think about the message! [heart]

Listen To Learn

TEACHER TALK: I often call on a student by saying,

❝Nolan, thank you for raising your hand,❞ thus encouraging others to do so. I may give a gentle reminder to someone who calls out, by saying, ❝Remember to raise your hand and I will call on you next.❞

STUDENTS RAISING THEIR HANDS: I often pick number sticks when asking questions but also use the traditional method: Raise your hand and wait to be called on.

ASKING QUESTIONS Before beginning a lesson, I give the students a purpose for listening. For example, I may say, "I want you to listen for rhyming words as we read this story." I lay out whatever my purpose is so that students can focus their thinking. Using open-ended questions avoids yes or no answers and encourages students to explain their thinking.

USING THE RESTROOM In my classroom, the restroom is located inside in the back. The rule is you don't have to ask to use it unless we are in a whole-group setting on the rug. If we are, students use our restroom signal: raising their hand and putting their thumb between their index and middle finger. This is purposely different from our question signal so that I can tell who has a question and who needs to go to the restroom. If they give me the signal and I nod at them they know they have my permission. Using this method I can keep my flow without interruption. I also feel not having to ask during the greater part of the day removes the mystique of doing something different than the group.

Restroom signal

When we are in the library, auditorium, or cafeteria, students use the hallway restrooms one at a time. In the beginning of the year they go with a partner to help them feel comfortable.

GETTING DRINKS Students are encouraged to get drinks in the morning before school and during recess breaks. I let students get drinks one at a time at other times of the day to avoid playing at the water fountain. Students use the sign for the letter *W* (making it with their index, middle, and ring finger) for "water."

Students in line for water fountain at recess

Water signal

PASSING OUT MATERIALS Another routine activity that students engage in daily is passing out materials. We have a system for this that releases me from the task and gives students a chance to be responsible and involved. My Helping Hand (see page 38) for the day selects one helper, and I split the pile of papers in half and give it to the helpers. The other students stand on the outside of our oval rug and then go to their desk once they receive a paper. Extra papers always go on my chair in the front of the room. Everyone knows where they are, so if someone is in the restroom and comes out, he or she can easily pick up the activity.

TEACHER TALK: When there is a variety of an item being passed around, students have learned that they may not ask for a specific color or selection. Our rule is

❝ You get what you get and you don't throw a fit. ❞

In the school library, I model how to look at a book.

HOW TO HANDLE A BOOK WHILE READING

It is better to explicitly teach to a kindergarten student simple things that you may take for granted. Students can be successful when they know your expectations. I teach my students what I expect to see during reading: students holding books right side up, turning the pages gently from the corner, looking at the pictures, and thinking about the story. Students are encouraged to share a book with a friend. They learn that books do not go under their bottoms or on their heads. We treasure books and treat them carefully.

TEACHER TALK: Describing what you see helps build students' self-esteem.

❝I see you are treating your independent reading book with respect by turning the pages gently from the corners.❞

Gavin and Brian, buddy-reading partners

Good reader strategies

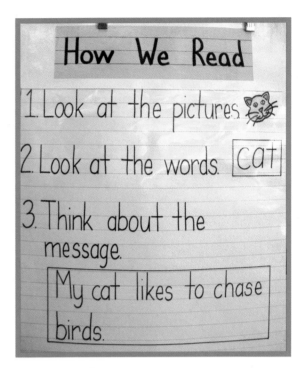

How we read

NAME ON PAPER Students are taught to write their names on the top left-hand corner of their paper. This helps me spot it easily on the page and encourages our concept-of-print chant, "Left to right, left to write, that is the way we read and write." For work that we hang in the classroom, I also write the student's name using a black marker on the top right-hand corner so that it stands out and parents can spot their child's work quickly.

A writing sample from the first day of school

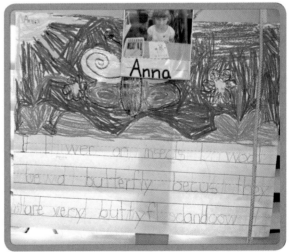

As soon as I have photos developed of all my students, I make photo name cards. Then I glue them to clothespins and use them to hang work for easy identification.

SHARP AND DULL PENCIL TINS: A volunteer sharpens the dull pencils to keep them in circulation.

SHARPENING PENCILS

Sharpening a pencil is a thrill for a kindergartener and can create a lot of noise in the classroom. In order to lessen the appeal of breaking a pencil just to sharpen it, I use two tins labeled Sharp and Dull. Students know if their pencil breaks, they put it in the Dull tin and take a new one from the Sharp tin. In the beginning of the year, if a student forgets what to do when a pencil breaks, I ask him or her a reflective question: "What do you do when your pencil breaks?" If the student still cannot remember, I ask a peer to guide the student to our pencil tins.

ACTIVITY TUBS

We have lots of activity tubs in our room and students follow one simple rule: Take out what you need, as you need it. They are not allowed to dump tubs. This helps us with cleanup and creates more floor space during math and choice time while we use tubs on the rug.

Activity tubs include items with a lot of small pieces, such as connecting blocks, magnets, a train set, and more.

Having students put the tub lid underneath the tub while it is in use is a great space saver.

SHARING MATERIALS In our classroom, students have their own desks with nameplates, crayon/pencil tubs, dictionaries, library books, alphabet charts, handwriting guides, and journals. Students develop a sense of ownership and responsibility from being in charge of their own work area. These same desks act as centers, where community materials from our classroom supply center are used at different times of the day. During shared times students are asked to take turns and be fair with materials. The beginning-of-the-year story *We Share Everything—* by Robert Munsch helps students understand the importance of sharing. We use the refrain from the book, "This is kindergarten. In kindergarten we share everything," throughout the year as a fun reminder that we are a team and we use the resources that we have together. Another story about helping and teamwork that kindergarteners always relate to is *The Selfish Crocodile* by Faustin Charles and Michael Terry.

Joey and Kali sharing crayons at the Listening Post

Harry and Shane at a math center exploring with dominoes

After finishing an assignment, Emilia reads independently.

WHAT TO DO WHEN YOU ARE DONE

"I'm done" rings in the ears of all teachers. Students will always finish assignments at different times. Teach your students what they can do after they complete an assignment. My students may read their library books, picture dictionaries, or work in their "anytime journal" (a blank composition book they may write or draw in when they have completed a whole-group assignment). If you choose an activity that is too inviting (for instance, blocks or toys), students may rush through their work in order to get to that activity. Choose their options wisely.

> **TEACHER TALK:** A good way to remind a small group of your expectations is to notice a student doing something right,
>
> 66 Nico, I like how you got your library book out when you finished your writing. 99

CLEANING UP Young children need direction when it comes to cleaning up. During the first week of school, I read *Max Cleans Up* by Rosemary Wells, and we have a discussion about how everything has a place, or a home, where it belongs. I have students model putting books and materials away in a calm, controlled manner. So much is happening at once during cleanup time that some students tend to lose self-control when they are asked to help. I am explicit with my directions: Students are to clean up quietly and treat materials with respect. I give positive feedback during this time to encourage students to follow role models. I also give immediate consequences if students throw materials or act out of control. Students who are not respecting materials lose their privilege of helping.

Students love cleaning their desks with shaving cream. After I give them a pump of cream they immediately start spreading the foam and writing or drawing in it. Next I pass out baby wipes. Then I ring the bell and students wipe their tables clean.

QUIET SIGNAL Every classroom needs a quiet signal that will help gain students' attention. I like to use auditory clap patterns or chants and short songs to regroup students. I also use this quick chant and then teach students the condensed version of it, which is simply "Give me five!": "My eyes are watching. My ears are listening. My mouth is closed. My feet are quiet. My hands are still."

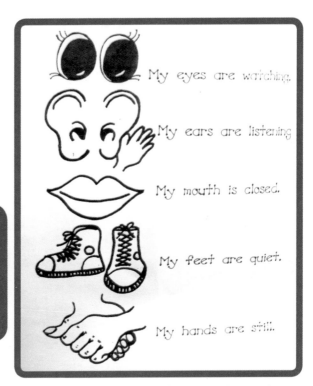

This chart, which helps students visualize and learn "Give me five!" in the beginning of the year, was made with the help of a poster maker.

FREEZE BELL When there is hustle and bustle in the room and I need everyone's attention I use my "freeze bell." Students know to freeze, put their eyes on the person with the bell, and put their hands on their head, shoulders, or knees. The chosen method may vary from year to year but should remain consistent throughout a given schoolyear. The Helping Hand rings the bell every day to give the signal to clean up and, once everyone is frozen, gives the message, "Please clean up quietly and come to the rug." I have one large bell that students know they use. There are several smaller bells throughout the room, which are only for me, that I use depending on where I am.

CIRCLE OF QUIET Young children naturally vocalize as they sound out words while writing. These sounds, as students stretch words, are developmentally appropriate. The Circle of Quiet game, played during our quiet writing time in the afternoon, discourages full conversations. I tell students that in this game, the goal is for no one to talk. We all put our index finger high up in the air and draw a large circle while slowly whispering, "circle of quiet." Then we begin our writing time. Someone who talks has broken the circle of quiet. I will remind him or her that we are playing the game. I write their number inside the circle on the board. Students who do not talk get chosen first for free choice time or receive an "I Caught the Wave" ticket (our school-wide recognition ticket for positive behavior).

Turning quiet time into a game makes it more fun and encourages cooperation.

VOICE LEVEL Young children use playground voices naturally. When you have 20-plus bodies in the room, this can become chaotic. In order to bring awareness to different volumes and voices we deliberately play around with voice. After I read the students the story *Millions of Cats* by Wanda Gag, we practice reading the silly refrain from the story with different voices:

> Hundreds of cats,
> Thousands of cats,
> Millions and billions and
> trillions of cats!

We use different voices, such as a loud voice, a whisper voice, an underwater voice (moving our finger over our lips as we speak), a telephone operator voice (pinching our nose), an opera voice (a singsong voice), and then no voice. Students giggle as they read the chant in different ways. Because of how silly the sounds are, this approach helps students learn that they can control their voice (including volume) and change it in a fun and entertaining way. This activity provides students with a frame of reference they can refer to as I model the voice I want them to use throughout the day.

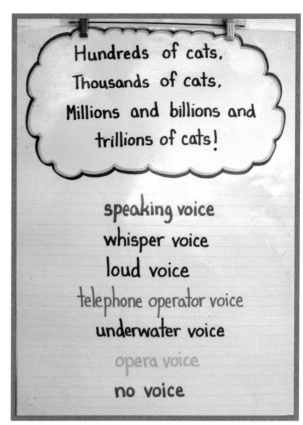

> **TEACHER TALK:** I model the behavior I want to see throughout my day and notice students who follow along,
>
> 66 Brayden, you are helping your whole group concentrate by remembering to use your whisper voice. 99
>
> During whole-group lessons, when I want to encourage participation, I am loud and animated. During literacy centers, when I want students to work quietly, I use a whisper voice.

Any silly refrain or chant that captures students' attention may be used to practice different voices and volume levels during the year. Fun chants help make this instruction memorable for students.

PLAYGROUND RULES AND PROCEDURES My kindergarten team and I have created rules and procedures which we all follow. This helps us stay consistent and provides students with clear expectations. In the beginning of the year, we review the rules outside on the playground so we can role-play and practice rules in an authentic setting.

I emphasize to students that we have rules to help keep everyone safe. Students can easily relate to the concept of safety.

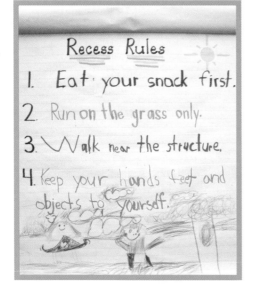

Recess Rules

1. Eat your snack first.

2. Run on the grass only.

3. Walk near the structure.

4. Keep your hands feet and objects to yourself.

Halfway through the school year, I always revisit the Recess Rules as an interactive writing activity.

Saying Good-Bye to Parents

First-day jitters are normal for kindergarten students. At our orientation before school begins, I let parents know that separation anxiety is eased if all parents give their child a hug, smile, and then wave good-bye at the classroom door. When parents linger, students become distracted and often emotionally torn. Let your classroom parents know that showing trust in the teacher will help their child gain confidence in their own ability to separate. If you do not have an orientation before the first day of school, you can direct the class to wave good-bye to their parents and then walk the students in the door.

Once inside the classroom, it is normal for some students to cry during the first few weeks of school. I have found the most effective way to regain the child's focus is to use distraction. I will go to the student next to him or her and start a conversation with that child.

Students in line waving good-bye

TEACHER TALK: When it's time to come into the classroom on the first day of school, to help students separate from their parents I say,

66 Boys and girls, wave good-bye to your parents. Good-bye moms and dads. Have a great day. We will. 99

On the first day of school I read *The Kissing Hand* by Audrey Penn, a beautiful story that describes the nervous feelings both students and parents have on this big day. The story teaches students a way to feel the love of their parents without being with them. Students make kissing hands and headbands and take them both home that day. This helps them remember to tell the story to their parents.

Beginning of the Year Checklist

1. Teach School Rules and Routines

- ❑ Playground rules and procedures
- ❑ Cafeteria rules and procedures
- ❑ Procedures for lunch money
- ❑ Homework policy
- ❑ Home Reading program
- ❑ Using the school library
- ❑ Obtaining a tardy slip from the office
- ❑ Emergency procedures

2. Establish Classroom Rules and Routines

- ❑ Classroom rules
- ❑ How to listen
- ❑ How to act on the rug
- ❑ How to handle materials
- ❑ How to work at centers
- ❑ How to read your books
- ❑ How to walk in line
- ❑ Walking routes
- ❑ Managing the noise level
- ❑ Getting students' attention
- ❑ Quiet signal
- ❑ Taking attendance
- ❑ Notes and correspondence from home
- ❑ Mailboxes
- ❑ Classroom volunteers
- ❑ Using the classroom library
- ❑ Using the restroom
- ❑ Asking for water
- ❑ Asking questions

3. Prepare Learning Materials

- ❑ Bulletin boards (paper and headings)
- ❑ Word Wall (put up letters A–Z)
- ❑ Morning Message
- ❑ Learning Centers (literacy, math, science)
- ❑ Journals
- ❑ Writing folders
- ❑ Projects and activities for first day
- ❑ Crayon tubs
- ❑ Home Reading envelopes
- ❑ Homework packets and envelopes

4. Prepare Management Materials

(Add students' names)
- ❑ Class number chart
- ❑ Class grids and lists
- ❑ Name tags
- ❑ Seating chart
- ❑ Temporary desk nameplates
- ❑ Name flash cards
- ❑ Helping Hands
- ❑ Literacy and Math Center groups
- ❑ Birthday items (calendar cakes and balloon cards)
- ❑ Homework folders
- ❑ Communication folders
- ❑ Number file folders for Student Portfolios

5. Plan Schedule and Lessons

- ❑ Daily schedule
- ❑ First week lesson plans
- ❑ Substitute plans
- ❑ Web page updates/ Important events

6. Assessments

- ❑ First day self-portrait
- ❑ Chart: This Is How I Write My Name
- ❑ First day writing sample
- ❑ Kindergarten skills (phonics, reading, math)
- ❑ Assessment Binders

7. Parent Information Packet

- ❑ Welcome letter
- ❑ Volunteer letter and survey
- ❑ Donation letter
- ❑ Supplies list
- ❑ Discipline plan
- ❑ Dismissal information sheet

8. New Students

- ❑ Parent information packet
- ❑ Homework packet and envelope
- ❑ Add student's name to necessary items

Discipline Plan

Teacher _____ Room _____

My goal is to teach students to take responsibility for themselves and their actions.

Rules

1. Follow directions the first time they are given.

2. Use quiet classroom voices.

3. Raise your hand to speak.

4. Keep hands, feet, and objects to yourself.

5. Use kind words and actions.

Rewards

1. Praise and positive feedback

2 Positive notes, awards, and messages to parents

3. Positive recognition from peers (cheers or compliments)

4. Privileges (extra recess or games)

5. Raffle tickets and prize box

6. Student of the Week

7. Class celebrations

Re-direction

1. "I message" to let students know what is expected

2. Proximity to the teacher

3. Special seating (seat students next to a role model)

4. Verbal reminders

5. Encouragement for effort

Consequences

1. Work time during recess or Free Choice

2. Teacher/Student Conference

3. Loss of one or more privileges

4. Parent contact (phone call, note home, or parent conference)

5. Behavior contract

Thank you for being a partner in your child's education. Please review this behavior plan with your child, sign, and return it by: _____

_____   _____
Student's Signature   Parent's Signature

CHAPTER 2

Organization

O rganization requires time and effort but will save you from the frustration of not being able to find what you need, when you need it, in the long run. When everything in your classroom has a place, both you and your students will know where to turn when you need something. You are the manager of your classroom, and devoting time to making sure everything has a system and a set home will keep your day running smoothly.

Teacher Planning

I map out a month of lesson plans at a time in my plan book. With all my guides and reference sheets at hand so that I know what concepts I need to cover, I list the texts I'm going to use and their purposes. Long-term planning gives me the chance to build on concepts and have clear goals for my students. In the beginning of the year I use our district modules for math, science, and English language development and fill in time frames for the units according to the pacing guides. I do the same thing for phonics and our units of inquiry. This provides me with a skeleton framework and pacing guide of my year, so that I know what I have covered and what is coming up.

PLAN BOOK AND YEARLONG PLAN I purchased a plan book organizer from an office supply store, which includes a notepad, pencil holder, and pocket folder with 25 clear-view pages. It contains my plan book and essential planning papers, such as state standards, a class roster, pacing guides, scope and sequence information, and the weekly bulletin. I make sure this organizer is fully stocked for use anywhere, at any time.

Flexibility is one of the keys in teacher planning. Be prepared, but remember there are constant interruptions to your day, such as school events, presentations, and visitors, that may require a change in plans.

One of my favorite time-saving tips for labeling my plan book came from a colleague. She taught me how to create computer-generated labels for my daily schedule that I now use to label my plan book for the year. She also advised not to apply labels before the schedule has been solidified. I also have a yearlong planning binder. This binder is a week-by-week guide of texts, activities, and centers that I use throughout the year. I refer to it as I plan for the specific needs of my class.

DAILY SCHEDULE Daily schedules vary depending on district requirements and special weekly periods such as physical education, library, and computer lab. Strive to achieve routine and structure. They are crucial for student success. Students feel at ease when they have a sense of what is coming next in their day. Think about the large blocks of time that you have and then plan accordingly. Also, it is critical in kindergarten to keep movement in mind. Students need to go back and forth between whole-group learning and independent practice and between sitting on the rug and working at seats. Another component to remember in planning is how learning builds. For instance, I do shared reading before independent reading and word study before writing. After keeping all these components in mind and creating your schedule, rest assured that if something is not flowing and you need to change it, you can.

IN- AND OUT-BOXES In-box items are my most current files, paperwork, and tasks that need to be completed. The out-box contains a plastic folder for photocopying, workroom mail, and office correspondence. I attend to these two trays on a daily basis. They keep my most important papers at my fingertips and ensure that I do not lose paperwork in my classroom.

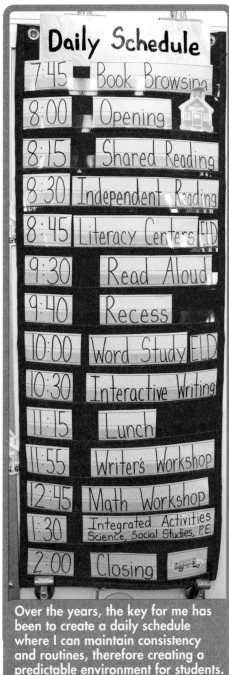

Over the years, the key for me has been to create a daily schedule where I can maintain consistency and routines, therefore creating a predictable environment for students.

IN- AND OUT-BOXES: These two trays sit side by side on the bookshelf next to my work table and are my lifeline to staying organized.

This clipboard helps keep my classroom running efficiently. It keeps all my most current important tasks in one place. I always bring it with me when I go to the supply room, office, or meetings.

TO-DO CLIPBOARD I am a quintessential list maker. Lists make me feel like I can let go of a pressing thought while still ensuring that the task will be accomplished. I used to write my to-do list on lined paper but then felt that categorizing my work would help me see more clearly what I needed to do. My personalized list on a clipboard takes the place of sticky notes and small random pieces of paper. I update my list weekly or as most of the tasks are accomplished.

SUBSTITUTE PLANS Detailed substitute plans are an investment you make for yourself. Once you put in the time to write out all the specifics that go into a typical day, put your plans in a clear-view pocket folder. This saves me time when I have to create lesson plans for a substitute. I leave my detailed plans along with a specific daily substitute plan with the schedule and information on materials and student groupings for the day. If you are out unexpectedly, your substitute will appreciate having a detailed plan for your day. I also include the following information in my substitute folder: photo name chart, class list, rules and discipline plan, daily schedule, student health information, seating chart, dismissal information, school map, and names of helpful students and people at the school.

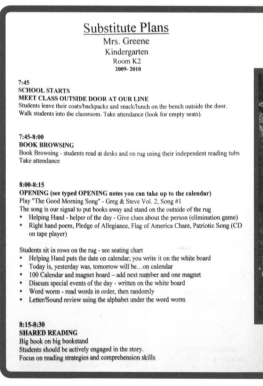

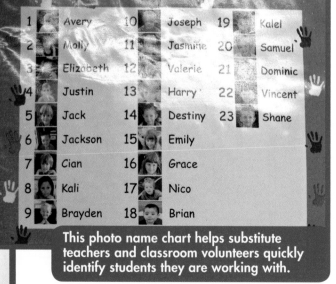

This photo name chart helps substitute teachers and classroom volunteers quickly identify students they are working with.

_____'s To-Do List

"Everything you do and say shows the world who you really are." —Oprah Winfrey

Things to Do	Office
1. _____	
2. _____	
3. _____	
4. _____	**Supplies**
5. _____	
6. _____	
7. _____	
8. _____	**Things to Buy**
9. _____	
10. _____	
11. _____	
12. _____	**Phone Calls**
13. _____	
14. _____	
15. _____	

Assessments	K Team	New Ideas
Interventions	**Computer**	**Personal**

Setting Up the Classroom

Throughout my years of teaching I have set up the classroom in many different ways, depending on the grade I was teaching and the structure of the room. Structural fixtures that cannot be moved, such as cabinets, windows, sinks, and doors, take precedence in planning.

THREE KEY ELEMENTS Begin by identifying your large-group area, making sure that you have the power position in the classroom. You want to be able to face the door and have the ability to see the rest of the room. After you designate your largest area, determine where you will work with students in small groups. Next, plan work areas or centers, depending on how you run your classroom.

There are three key elements to keep in mind as you set up your room: point of use, pathways, and visibility.

Point of Use: Put items where they are needed. This may sound logical, but sometimes you need to be creative in order to find the space you need, where you need it.

Pathways: Keep pathways wide, open, and flowing.

Visibility: Make sure there are no hiding places. You should be able to scan the room from your small-group work table.

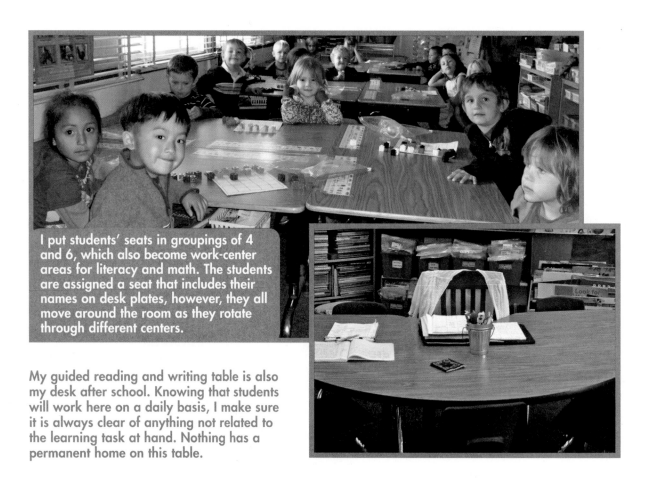

I put students' seats in groupings of 4 and 6, which also become work-center areas for literacy and math. The students are assigned a seat that includes their names on desk plates, however, they all move around the room as they rotate through different centers.

My guided reading and writing table is also my desk after school. Knowing that students will work here on a daily basis, I make sure it is always clear of anything not related to the learning task at hand. Nothing has a permanent home on this table.

I consider the reading center to be a key learning area. I wanted mine to be prominent so I placed it in the middle of the room.

READ-ALOUD DISPLAY: When students, parents, or visitors first walk in my door, they get an immediate idea of what we are studying from the read-aloud display. I take advantage of the end of my art counter, which is located near the door, where I place thematic fabric and books displayed on easel stands.

FLOOR PLAN Using grid paper, sketch out the fixed structures in your room, then use labels made from different-sized sticky notes to play around with different ways you might organize your classroom. The floor plan below shows my most recent classroom layout. Student desks double as the various learning centers.

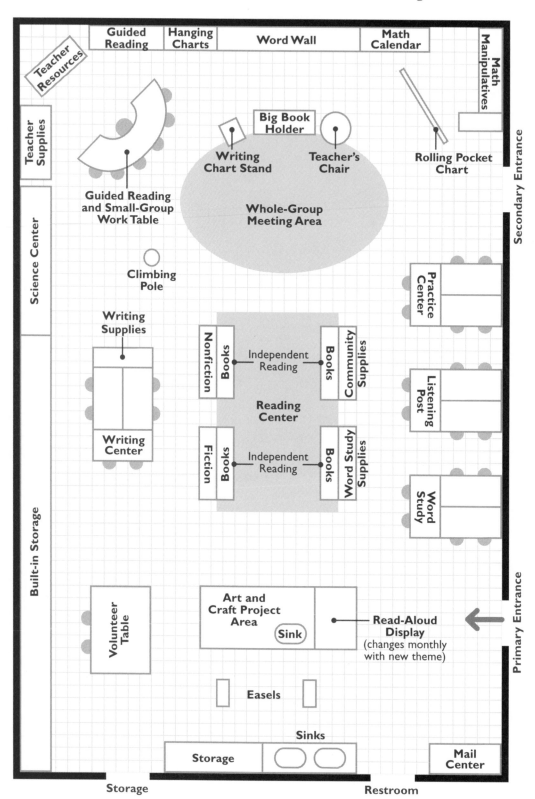

PROJECT BAGS AND THEME TUBS

I use extra-large plastic zipper bags to store all my projects. I keep the project sample, stencils, and all project-related materials together in the bag. This saves me from having to look for parts of a project. I keep all my project bags in theme tubs. I have tubs for literacy, math, and science. I usually start planning for an upcoming month in the middle of the previous month. This gives me time to photocopy papers I need and gives my volunteers plenty of time to prepare materials for students. By planning ahead, I am better able to use the help of my volunteers and avoid having to rush to get something ready.

Using tubs to store units has been a great timesaver for me and has helped me with organization. All my teaching materials and projects have a home. I chose not to store my read-aloud books in the tubs because it would cut off easy access to them and also make the tubs too heavy.

CHAPTER 3

Classroom Management

Classroom management is the glue that will keep your classroom together. It is a crucial element in best utilizing learning time and increasing students' time on task. With good systems in place for managing students, your routines will flow and your day should run smoothly. Students will respond to methods that are consistent. This will help create a predictable environment for them, which will lead to increased comfort for learning. Teaching students about proper classroom behavior and how to self-regulate is one of the goals in kindergarten.

Taking Attendance

The way I take attendance has changed several times over the years, depending on my classroom management and how our morning begins. I like to link it to a learning activity. The following are different ways I have taken attendance:

ASSIGNED SEATS A simple method I use is assigning students seats in the classroom and beginning the day with Book Browsing or Independent Reading. I simply check to see which seats are empty and take attendance.

POCKET CHART WITH PHOTOS In years that I do not assign seats for individual students, I use a rolling pocket chart with students' photo name cards. At the top of the pocket chart I have a sentence strip that says, "I am glad you are here today." Students move their photo card from below a line of stickers to the top portion of the chart.

QUESTION-OF-THE-DAY GRAPH Sometimes I use a Question-of-the-Day graph that hangs outside my door. I tell parents about it and teach students how to interact with it on the first day of school. Every day, students answer a new question by moving a clothespin labeled with their name to represent their answer on a graph. The expectation is that they do this before coming into the classroom. When it is time for attendance, simply looking at who has not moved their clip from the side of the chart to an answer (and checking the room for the student) is all it takes. The graph can be used later as a math warm-up activity, such as a review of counting or vocabulary (*more, less, same*).

Day-to-Day Student Organization

NUMBERING STUDENTS

This management strategy, which I learned from Rick Morris's book *New Management Handbook*, has been monumental in saving me time and energy. Using the class roster on the first day of school, I assign each student a number for the year. You may want to wait longer if you suspect your roster may change in the beginning of the year. A number chart is created, which the children and I use as a reference throughout the year.

Kindergarten students quickly learn their own numbers as well as those of their peers. There are several additional benefits to using numbers:

- I call on students to answer questions by drawing number sticks.

- It's an efficient way to dismiss students from the rug.

- It helps determine ownership of items that are not put away.

- All students quickly learn these numbers!

1	Avery	13		Harry
2	Molly	14		Destiny
3	Elizabeth	15		Emily
4	Justin	16		Grace
5	Jack	17		Nico
6	Jackson	18		Brian
7	Cian	19		Kalel
8	Kali	20		Samuel
9	Brayden	21		Dominic
10	Joseph	22		Vincent
	Jasmine	23		Shane
	Valerie			

Class Numbers

1. Avery
2. Molly
3. Elizabeth
4. Justin
5. Jack
6. Jackson
7. Cian
8. Kali
9. Brayden
10. Joey (Joseph)
11. Jasmine
12. Valerie
13. Harry
14. Destiny
15. Emily
16. Grace
17. Nico
18. Brian
19. Kalel
20. Samuel
21. Dominic
22. Vincent
23. Shane

NUMBER CHARTS: I place a variety of number charts throughout the room for those who are assisting or visiting to use.

Mrs. Greene Room K2 2009-2010				
1. Avery	2. Molly	3. Elizabeth	4. Justin	5. Jack
6. Jackson	7. Cian	8. Kali	9. Brayden	10. Joseph
11. Jasmine	12. Valerie	13. Harry	14. Destiny	15. Emily
16. Grace	17. Nico	18. Brian	19. Kalel	20. Samuel
21. Dominic	22. Vincent	23. Shane		

Student grids are one of the most used, multifunctional teacher tools in my classroom.

CLASS GRIDS Class grids are used as assessment tools as well as for management. They serve as a nice layout for class information. Volunteers use them routinely as a checklist. The same grid may be reused several times. This seemingly simple form is multifunctional and has many practical uses in the classroom. These include:

- Class overview for scores on assessments
- Conferring notes (reading, writing, math)
- Volunteer checklist (calling students for projects)
- Collection checklist (school photographs, permission slips, donations)

Behavior Incentives

THE HELPING HAND GAME We play this elimination game each morning to help determine the helper for the day. I give clues about the student, incorporating important language and reinforcing academic vocabulary and phonics skills. We begin while students are still standing after the Good Morning song. Students sit down if the clue I give them is not about them, until one student remains standing. This student helps pass out papers, runs errands in the classroom, rings the bell to give the message to clean up, and selects other students to help as needed. He or she also becomes calendar helper and line leader, which affords me a few minutes of one-on-one time for personal conversation while walking to lunch each day. The Helping Hand takes home a sharing tin at the end of the day. (See page 88 for more about the sharing tin.) This position is always in high demand. Students know that I select names randomly. This makes it fair and I often say, "It is random because you are all good helpers." As students take a turn, I move their hand from the Helping Hands side of a small pocket holder to the "I helped in K2!" side. After everyone has had a turn, I move all the hands back to the Helping Hands side and everyone has another chance to be selected.

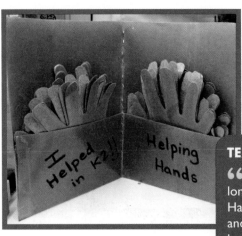

TEACHER TALK: Helping Hand clues sound like this:

❝Today my Helping Hand is someone who has the long A sound in his or her name. Today my Helping Hand is someone who has the long A sound in his name, and he is a boy. Today my Helping Hand is someone who has the long A sound in his name, he is a boy, and he is wearing plaid.❞

Typically, after three or four clues, my Helping Hand is revealed.

MYSTERY SENTENCE As a whole-class reward, students earn a letter when they work cooperatively and follow directions as a group. The mystery sentence can be anything you decide upon. My mystery sentences include:

- Working together you earned a class party!
- Congratulations, Kindergarteners!

Varying whole-group rewards motivates students to work together cooperatively. I use the mystery sentence chart after our class has earned a Marble Jar Party to excite and motivate them. Students love trying to guess the mystery sentence.

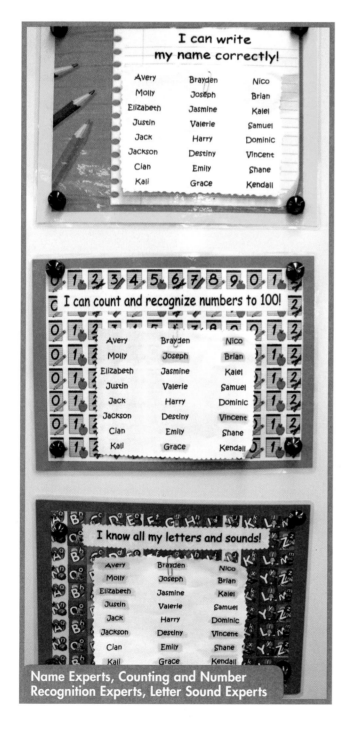

Name Experts, Counting and Number Recognition Experts, Letter Sound Experts

EXPERT CHARTS These charts serve multiple purposes. They help me keep track of who has mastered basic skills and aid in identifying peer tutors. Students who need more time to learn are given extra practice time and often work with their peers. Becoming a peer helper motivates students to continue practicing. Kids helping kids can be a powerful approach. In our classroom, everyone's a teacher.

Classroom Management

FIVE-MINUTE NOTICE This technique helps students come to terms with the fact that a transition time is approaching. I ring our freeze bell and say, "Five minutes until clean up. Finish up what you are doing." I can't emphasize enough how much this simple reminder helps prepare students to switch gears.

TICKET TO LEAVE Before students are dismissed for recess or to line up for lunch, they have to give me their "ticket to leave." This entails a verbal response to a question of my choosing. I use this time as a quick review of anything we are learning: letters and sounds, numbers, story characters, color words, and so on. I purposely call students I know can answer correctly first. This gives my students who need extra practice a little extra review on a daily basis. I keep the last few students who don't know the answers and do a quick review of the learning with this small group.

Ringing a bell to signal a five-minute notice gives the students who need time to mentally prepare before transitioning to a new activity a chance to be successful. These students will be less reluctant to stop what they are doing if they are given time to process.

The Ticket to Leave builds a quick, daily review of important concepts into our daily schedule.

Formal Discipline/Behavior Plans

RULES, REWARDS, AND CONSEQUENCES

A classroom discipline plan is required at most schools. Rules are modeled and role-played during the first month of school. When we have trouble with a rule, we review it as a class. I use a problem-solving wheel that helps students learn new ways to deal with different situations. I also consciously slow down my directions and make sure I am very explicit and clear while giving directions. This helps students to be successful.

Holding students accountable for their choices and behavior is at the foundation of my behavior system. I find when students are expected to make good choices and think before they act, they are able to rise to the occasion.

We are Kindergarteners
We share everything.
We are kind.
We take turns.
We listen to each other.
We work together.
We help each other.
We use good manners.
We do our best and forget the rest!

APOLOGIZE
SHAKE HANDS AND TAKE TURNS
GO TO ANOTHER GAME
WALK AWAY
COUNT TO TEN TO COOL OFF 10
CLASS MEETING AGENDA
TELL THEM TO STOP
USE AN "I" MESSAGE
STOP

TEACHER TALK: Cuing students with questions, such as **"Where should you be right now?"** or **"What should you be doing?"** provide students the opportunity to problem-solve and redirect themselves.

POSITIVE NOTES AND PHONE CALLS HOME

A positive note home is a powerful tool for teachers. Every child does something positive in the course of the day. Highlighting the good choice a student makes encourages the child to repeat the behavior. I make sure that each child receives a personal "happy" note during the first few weeks of school. To motivate students who were having a hard time making good choices, I display the notes in a pocket chart so that they are visible to them throughout the day. Students know I really want to give their families positive feedback but that they have to earn the note by making a good choice. This simple note sets the wheels in motion for all students in the class to strive to do what they know is right. I also make positive phone calls, which only take a moment, but are appreciated by parents and also have a positive ripple effect on students' classroom behavior.

Emily,
You wrote a beautiful message to Noah today. Your illustrations were beautiful also. You are a very talented and caring young girl. I know he will find your card very special. It was obviously made with love.
I am so proud of you!
love, Mrs. Greene

Great job!
Emily
A+

11/17/09

BEHAVIOR CLIPBOARD This clipboard is used to record information about both positive and negative behavior. A grid on the top helps me track positive notes and phone calls home. This ensures all students receive encouragement about their good behavior. Negative behaviors are also recorded as well as what type of parent communication was made. The recorded information serves as a tool for quickly spotting patterns and ensures clear communication between school and home. The first month of school is the busiest month for recording information. By getting parents involved immediately, negative behaviors tend to diminish very quickly. Students are acutely aware that they are accountable for their choices and behavior in the classroom. A Beginning of the Year progress report developed by our grade-level team goes home at the end of September. A parent signature is required and the form is returned so that close home-school communication is maintained. When there is a more recurring behavior pattern, I make a weekly contract with the student and his or her parents. The student works on improving one behavior at a time.

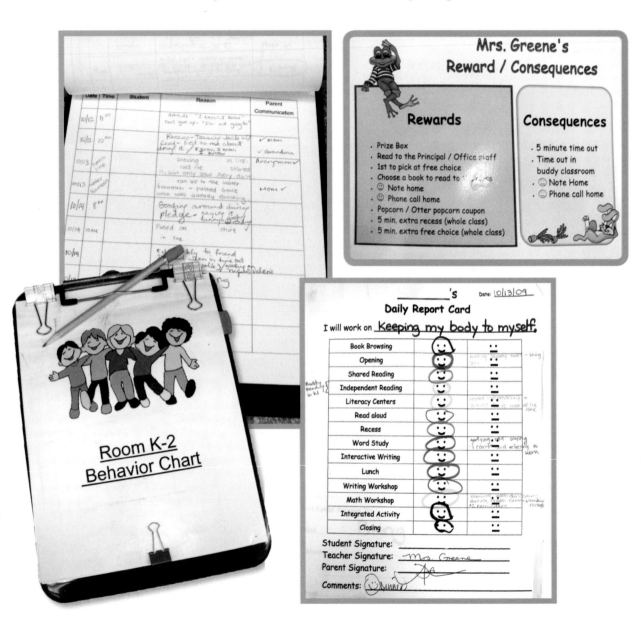

A Daily Report Card records how the student progressed throughout the day (focusing on just one target behavior). A consequence and reward menu is used at school, and a home-based reward/consequence plan is created by the parents. The child quickly learns that his or her teacher and parents are on the same page and are working together to help improve behavior.

CLASS MOTTO, CHANT, AND PLEDGE When you want students to remember an important concept, a chant will do the trick.

- Our Class Motto is "Do your best!"

- Our Class Chant is "You get what you get and you don't throw a fit." (This chant has saved me from whining and tantrums more than once!)

- Our Class Pledge is "My hands are for helping, not for hurting."

TEACHER TALK: When students are almost finished cleaning up their centers for our read-aloud story time, I start singing this short song (to the tune of "If You're Happy and You Know It"):

❝If you're ready for a story, find a seat.

If you're ready for a story, find a seat.

If you're ready for a story, check your hands and then your feet.

If you're ready for a story, find a seat.❞

Students know that when I am done with the song I expect them to be gathered on the rug. This encourages them not to linger and to finish putting materials away quickly.

CHAPTER 4

Literacy: Whole-Group Learning

My whole-group meeting area with an oval-shaped alphabet rug is the heart of my classroom. I selected this rug specifically for its shape, since teaching in a circle encourages communication and participation from students.

Students transition back and forth from areas in the room to the rug throughout the day. We sit in rows during reading and writing lessons and on the outside of the oval for math. Students have assigned spots on the rug while in rows, depending on height, compatibility, and special needs. Lots of learning and discussion take place in this area, so all the resources I need are within reach. This way, I do not have to go somewhere else in the room for supplies while I am teaching. During lessons, I will often refer to previous learning that has been recorded on charts and the word wall, or in books that are all positioned in this critical area.

Reading and Writing

Whole-group learning experiences, such as shared reading, shared writing, interactive and modeled writing, word study, and sharing of students' own reading and writing, take place on the alphabet rug.

SHARED READING Reading together is a joyful experience for kindergarteners. Shared reading books provide the opportunity for students to become involved in the reading process and learn the strategies readers use to learn to read. My shared reading books are stored in large wooden boxes and are sorted by month. I also have separate categories for math and science. For books that come with a guide, I tape a large envelope to the back cover of the book in which the guide is stored. This ensures that I can find the guide immediately.

I pull my big books for the month out of the bookshelf and put them next to my shared reading big-book stand for easy access. Reading-strategy cards with visual clues are laminated and made into giant magnets, which I can pull off my big-book stand during a lesson. I keep a variety of pointers, Wikki Stix, highlighting tape, and word swatters (fly swatters with the middle cut out) on my big book stand. I also bring

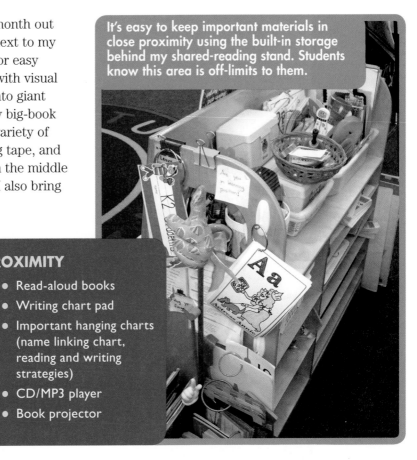

It's easy to keep important materials in close proximity using the built-in storage behind my shared-reading stand. Students know this area is off-limits to them.

MATERIALS IN CLOSE PROXIMITY

- Word worm (sight words)
- Word wall
- Rolling pocket chart
- Big-book stand
- Long and short pointers
- Flash cards (names, colors, alphabet, sight words, blends, number words)
- Read-aloud books
- Writing chart pad
- Important hanging charts (name linking chart, reading and writing strategies)
- CD/MP3 player
- Book projector

Students practice sequencing a sentence

Have you seen my cat ?

up related props and realia to help students connect to the text. I use my rolling pocket chart to do shared readings of poems and songs, and I prepare story map framework charts to support reading.

Look for opportunities to help students connect to text. During this shared reading of *Five Little Monkeys* on the first day of school, I noticed Jackson had an extra-large bandage on his forehead. He was excited to come to the front of the room to model for his peers how he bumped his head!

We use a stuffed toy to designate the speaker during oral language development before or after a story.

Dominic working on the -at family during an interactive writing/word study lesson

INTERACTIVE WRITING Interactive writing, a teacher-guided activity, helps students step by step through the writing process. Everyone is involved. Whiteboards, dry-erase markers, and felt erasers are handy, in a basket near the main walking path to the rug. Students form a line and pick up one of each item for the lesson. Once they get to the rug, they begin practicing sight words until all of the students are on the rug.

When we are ready to begin the lesson, I ask students to "park their pens and erasers in their driveways" (the area in front of them). We then begin our discussion, which always precedes the lesson. During this activity, one student will come up to write words on our chart while the other students practice on their whiteboards. I put up a letter-writing guide so that students can see how letters are formed, and I model each letter, verbalizing its shape and formation. To help students see the correct letter formation,

I drew "head, belt, and toe" lines on top of my magnetic writing board with a permanent marker.

During the lesson, students put their pens in ready position (in the air) as they finish each letter. This enables us to stay together as a group. The process is slow, but students benefit greatly from it. They learn how writers create ideas, formulate sentences, form words, and use sounds in words. They also learn about print concepts, such as spacing, sizing, and punctuation. Under our writing easel, I keep all the supplies that I need: pens, scented markers, a dictionary, white correction tape, rulers, a spaceman, pointers, and several "Mr. Letterman" guides that I attach to the chart paper before we use it.

TEACHER TALK: To help students stay together as a group during interactive writing lessons, I use these key phrases:

❝Park your pens and erasers❞ and
❝Show me the ready position.❞

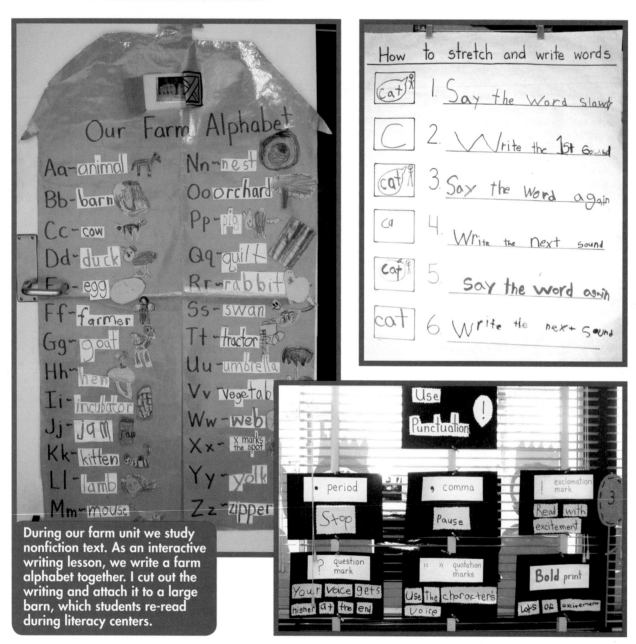

During our farm unit we study nonfiction text. As an interactive writing lesson, we write a farm alphabet together. I cut out the writing and attach it to a large barn, which students re-read during literacy centers.

Word Study

WORD WALL Our word wall begins with magnetic A–Z die-cut letters on the whiteboard. In September, as we learn letters and sounds, we begin to build words by blending two or three letters together. This supports both our phonics and reading goals for the beginning of the year. For example, after we learn the letters and sounds for *M* and *O*, we build the word *mom*. We build the word with magnetic letters and put it on the word wall. I purposely do not add a picture, because I want the students to rely on looking at the letters to read the word. This encourages students to apply what they learn and make sense of why they are learning their letters and sounds. The word wall grows as we learn more letters and sounds. Our word wall becomes an extension of our phonics study.

The word wall transforms throughout the year, according to the needs of the students. When we study nutrition, students bring in food labels, and we use the word wall to put up the food labels we can read. In January, after students have learned letters and sounds solidly, I take down the magnetic alphabet and put up blend cards, which we refer to when we do our weekly word family work.

From letters to words

Word study using key consonant digraphs

Word worm

SIGHT WORDS Sight words are learned using a word worm. We start the year with just the worm's head. I tell the students he is a word worm and ask them to guess what he likes to eat. I get all kinds of great responses from this question. After making some rumbling noises, we put up our new word. I use the Dolch word list (a list of sight words that are most frequently found in children's books) and put up a total of 25 words (one a week) during the first 25 weeks of school. We read these words as part of our morning opening and play games with them. We look for letters in words and words in words, and say rhymes with them. We clap them and spell them in the air, from head to toe. We "write" them on our hands, legs,

Word family charts

and rug. We spell them with our eyes closed.

I tell students that our goal is to get them off the wall and into our brains. We learn them inside out and as quick as a snap. Students also work on these words as they are on the first of 11 lists in my Home Reading program. As students progress in Home Reading, they continue to practice additional sight words at their own pace.

MORE WORD WORK Another important grouping of words is the students' names. During the first weeks of school, our class creates a name linking chart. It is written in alphabetical order and is hung directly above our writing chart. We use this chart throughout the year as we reference names during our learning.

Color words are a word grouping that stays up all year long. Our color words are on the cabinets near our painting easels and art center.

During the second half of the year, once we begin learning word families, they are posted on shape charts and stay up as a reference tool.

Bulletin Boards

Our bulletin board display changes on a monthly basis to reflect our unit of study. I use students' art and/or writing to create the display. Our themes help students make connections in their learning. Our literature, art, social studies, health, and science are interconnected with each theme. My monthly themes do not guide my curriculum; instead, they provide a focus for them. Parents, family, and visitors know what we are learning about before they even enter our room. The themes are as follows:

- September: Myself
- October: Cats, bats, and pumpkins
- November: Harvest
- December: Gingerbread Man
- January: Fairy tales
- February: Friendship
- March: Farm; Spring
- April: Insects; Plants
- May: Ocean
- June: Change

I add supplemental themes to a secondary bulletin board. For example, in September I put up the setting from *Chicka Chicka Boom Boom* so that we can add our names to the tree after we read the story. I keep this up until December, when we are learning about story elements such as retelling, characters, and setting. Together we create a Gingerbread Man mural. This mural remains through our fairy tale unit and then is replaced by a world map so that we can map our travels with Flat Stanley. Lastly, we end with an ocean mural.

Another option is to create a writing wall to put up students' monthly writing samples. Depending on your purpose, you may choose to add to students' work, so that over the year it becomes like a wall portfolio, or update it as students progress. I use the students' monthly writing samples for our class memory books, which I add to each month, so I keep only the most recent writing on the wall. I use binder clips to hang the writing and have a photo name card for quick identification of student work. Other options include using laminated paper as backing or clear-view pocket holders to contain students' writing.

CHAPTER 5

Literacy: Independent and Small-Group Learning

Independent learning takes place in the context of a literacy center. Each literacy center is housed within a bookshelf, which stores the materials related to that center. Baskets that sit on top of the shelves hold the specific teacher-planned weekly task. Students are responsible for taking out and putting away materials. My goal is for students to establish independence and responsibility so that I am able to pull students from different groups for guided reading.

Literacy Centers

Literacy center groups are heterogeneous, mixed-ability groups. Each group of four students is assigned a different center each day. After students complete the center, they read five books from their independent reading tub and record the titles in their reading log. If they complete that task, they may choose their next learning activity from a "Got Choices" chart. Students rotate through each center over the course of a week. Groups are changed every four to six weeks so that students have the opportunity to work with new friends.

We quickly review these five rules every day before center time.

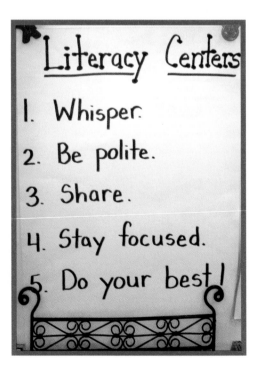

Literacy Centers

1. Whisper.
2. Be polite.
3. Share.
4. Stay focused.
5. Do your best!

Emily practices reading color words.

Vincent writes in his journal.

I take time to strategically plan groups of students who will work together. This helps with management during center time. I consider students' academic abilities and social needs.

PRACTICE CENTER The task at this center is determined by the needs of the class. Assignments include alphabet work, name practice, handwriting, sight word books, and literacy theme projects.

Students listening to *All About You* by Catherine and Laurence Anholt

LISTENING POST Every week, students listen to a new story and respond to it in some way. In the beginning of the year, students copy the title, rate the book using a happy face system, and draw a picture of their favorite part of the story. As they progress, students add a written response. An alphabet practice sheet is photocopied on the back of each response sheet. Once they have completed their listening post response, students practice writing the alphabet using rainbow writing, going over each letter with crayons in all the colors of the rainbow (red, then orange, and so on).

WORD STUDY CENTER Students practice many word-building activities at this center. Resources include the following:

- Whiteboards, dry-erase markers, and felt erasers
- Magnetic writing board and tracing sheets
- Magnetic letters
- Foam letters
- Sight word cards and books
- Picture and noun word cards
- Alphabet books

Working on the *–an* family

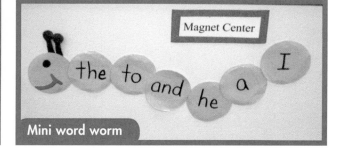

Mini word worm

The library is set up to encourage independence. All books are labeled with a numbered sticker that corresponds to the tub that houses it.

READING CENTER

The reading center is in the middle of our classroom because reading is at the core of all our learning. Our large reading center has a variety of books: big books, author sets, fiction, nonfiction, magazines, dictionaries, shared reading sets, and independent reading books. Books face out so that the covers attract the student's eye. To make the reading center more inviting, I have also included cushions, large animal pillows, and pointers.

WRITING CENTER

During literacy centers, I assign writing tasks. This center is open again in the afternoon as a free choice center and has always been one of the most popular areas in the room. Students love to create all types of products at this area. I think the availability of many resources and the ability to make their own choices entices students to want to write. Our center includes the following:

I show students that I value their writing by posting the notes, letters, and cards they write to me on a large bulletin board in the classroom.

- Small blank books (made with wrapping paper covers)
- Shape books
- Paper (lined, blank, letter format, colored)
- Markers and crayons
- Envelopes
- Word baskets
- Art tools (stencils, texture boards)
- How-to-draw books
- Stapler, hole punch, and yarn

Emi and Matthew at the writing center, drawing and labeling insects in their science journals

Students are eager to share their writing using our microphone, which I purchased as an inexpensive karaoke machine.

Reading an alphabet puzzle

GAMES AND PUZZLES CENTER

Students practice the alphabet using dry-erase boards first and then may choose from selected games or puzzles at the center. Every week I put out 2 or 3 activities that match the focus of our learning. Students use the whole-group oval rug as their work area. Tasks include alphabet and word work, sequencing cards, puzzles, rhyming activities, phonics games, and sight word games.

Writing sight words in a sand tub

Small-Group Work

The same table serves as my desk, assessment area, and small-group area. Because students join me here throughout the day for guided reading, guided writing, word study, or English language development, I never store paperwork here. I keep book club tubs, guided reading books, and other resources I may need for small-group lessons directly behind my table for quick and easy access.

When I call reading groups to my table, I invite them to come to a book club. The book club tubs and guided reading books are stored within reach.

CHAPTER 6

Math, Science, Art, and More

Kindergarteners love hands-on learning and it is greatly incorporated in these subject areas. Whole-group mini-lessons are typically followed by experiential, independent practice using manipulatives and materials that foster creativity. Students become involved through project-based lessons where they are required to apply what they have learned.

Mathematics

Our district and state math standards require that all kindergarteners learn multiple strands of math. Students are exposed to sorting and classifying, patterns, graphing, number sense, matching and counting, geometry and equal parts, money, measurement, time, and addition and subtraction. To support learning I add a routine that supports the module we are studying to my daily calendar. One of my overarching goals is to help students develop flexibility in problem solving. I do this by putting a strong emphasis on requiring students to explain their thinking.

MATH CALENDAR Our math calendar is part of our opening routine. This creates predictability and allows for repetition, both of which enhance student learning. Basic math calendar activities remain standard, while special activities are added each month, depending on our math unit. This allows me to keep the calendar learning time between 5 and 10 minutes. Our morning calendar routine includes the following:

- **Counting the days to date on the monthly calendar.**
- **Today is (day of week, month, date, year).**
- **Review concept of today/yesterday/tomorrow:**

    Today is_____.

    Yesterday was _____.

    Tomorrow will be_____.

- **Count the number of days in school:**

    Count the 100 chart by ones, adding one number for each day in school.

    Add one magnet for each day to the ten frames chart, then count by tens.

- **Weather chant and graph:**

  The whole class claps and recites the weather chant, while our Helping Hand shakes maraca:

  "Weather, weather all together, what will the weather be?

  Is it sunny? Is it windy? Is it rainy? Is it cloudy? Is it foggy?"

  We use hand motions for each type of weather. The Helping Hand looks out the window and says, "Today the weather is _____."

  We add the correct symbol to the weather graph and then compare the different types of weather. Which type of weather have we had the most of? Which type of weather have we had the least of? Are any the same?

MATH POCKET CHART I make sure to have key vocabulary available for students to reference, which we routinely review during math lessons. Visual examples help students with understanding new academic terms and provide a frame of reference during a lesson.

Teaching students the word *coincidence* as Joey was randomly selected to be Helping Hand on the 25th of March and he was wearing a jersey with a 25 on it!

TEACHER TALK: I use questions that require students to give me an explanation of their work:

❝Show me what you are thinking…❞

❝How do you know that? Please show us…❞

❝Who saw it differently?❞

❝Who can explain?❞

❝What would happen if…❞

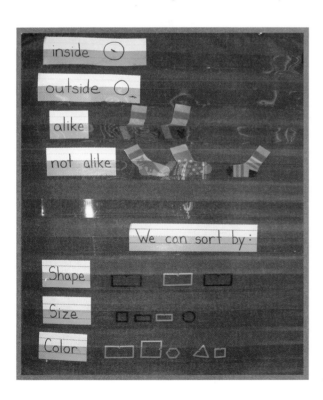

Math vocabulary and concepts

MATH CENTERS I manage math centers differently than literacy centers. During math centers, students work at their seats and the math tubs rotate. Students go to math centers four times each week. For easy cleanup, students put math center materials in their respective tubs and put the tubs in the math cupboard. The system promotes independence. Sometimes students use math tubs on the rug to reduce noise created when they use manipulatives on tables.

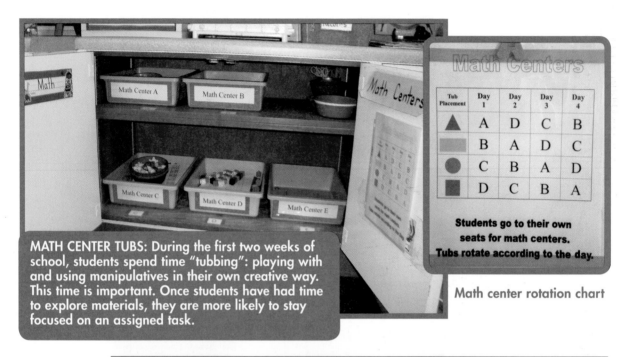

MATH CENTER TUBS: During the first two weeks of school, students spend time "tubbing": playing with and using manipulatives in their own creative way. This time is important. Once students have had time to explore materials, they are more likely to stay focused on an assigned task.

Math Centers

Tub Placement	Day 1	Day 2	Day 3	Day 4
▲	A	D	C	B
▬	B	A	D	C
●	C	B	A	D
■	D	C	B	A

Students go to their own seats for math centers. Tubs rotate according to the day.

Math center rotation chart

Grace checking her yellow, green, blue, red (ABCD) pattern

Kendall adding links to number cards during math centers

Manipulatives are stored in tubs at the math calendar area. They are used for whole-group lessons as well as math learning centers.

ESTIMATION JAR

The estimation jar routine begins after each student has had a turn to be the ESP (Extra Special Person). This is typically in late February. The student of the week takes home our estimation jar (with directions attached to it) and returns it with 20–40 items to share with the class. Before estimating, we use a helper jar to visualize a group of 10 of whatever object is brought.

Students always look forward to this activity. We have enjoyed treats, shells, balloons, stickers, bouncy balls, rulers, erasers, rings, and so on, which excite students and pique interest.

The estimation jar routine provides students with important practice in visualizing groups of 10, estimating, and matching and counting.

Science

Our science center provides students with a place to probe, wonder, and learn. Hands-on experiences, realia, and exploration are the keys to these centers. I continually search for real-world items that relate to my curriculum. If you know your curriculum well, you can always be on the lookout for deals at discount stores, garage sales, library book sales, thrift stores, or any other place you might be. Hands-on materials are used to support our learning goals.

We always connect these experiences to literacy. For example, students have a science journal in which they record observations and learning during literacy centers.

Mr. Bell talking to students about our Western toads, Bill and Ted

Ted

Live specimens in my classroom typically include red worms, earthworms, pill bugs, goldfish, guppies, and snails.

We transformed our outdoor sandbox into a garden by removing the sand and adding soil. Our kindergarten classes included personal touches, such as pots, hand-painted rocks, and signs.

GARDEN There are so many resources available for gardening with children. The California School Garden Network offers a free resource guide for teachers called *Gardens for Learning*. It can be requested at www.csgn.org. We also received a donation of a greenhouse. Local nurseries have donated plants, soil, and gardening tools to help us get started. Parents also donate toward a garden fund, which provides us with enough money to purchase seeds, starter plants, soil, compost, and other supplies at the beginning of the year. Garden experiences are ongoing. Our garden provides us with an outdoor classroom as we integrate gardening with literature, writing, math, science, and social studies lessons.

A GARDEN DOESN'T HAVE TO BE OUTDOORS

You can provide students with a garden experience on any scale you choose, and it doesn't have to occur outdoors. There are mini-greenhouse planters that are relatively inexpensive (available at most garden centers). This can provide the opportunity for students to plant seeds and observe them growing inside the classroom.

Social Studies

Our state history–social science content standards include a focus on the behaviors of a good citizen, national and state symbols, community helpers, maps and map skills, understanding and sequencing temporal order using a calendar, and learning about major holidays and events and important people in American history. These standards integrate nicely into the curriculum and I teach them during reading, writing, and math periods using text, writing, and calendar activities. Following rules, sharing, taking turns, and knowing the consequences when rules are broken are all social studies standards that fit naturally into every kindergarten day.

LETTER TO THE PRESIDENT When I teach letter writing we use interactive writing to scribe a letter to the president. Students give the president their suggestions on ways to help the country. My students are always thrilled to receive their reply from the White House. We have also written to the Queen of England. She, too, will write back!

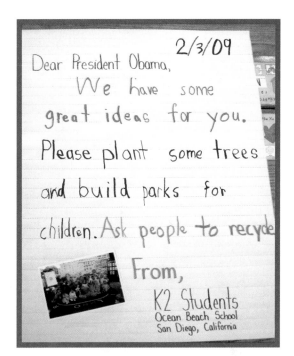

Kindergarten students can make a difference.

FLAT STANLEY During our study of Friendship we read the story *Flat Stanley* by Jeff Brown. In this story Stanley is flattened when a bulletin board falls on top of him. His parents take advantage of his flattened state and send him in an envelope to visit friends far away. My students learn about letter writing and make paper doll cutouts of themselves that we send to friends and family throughout the world. We enclose a note explaining the activity and ask that a small souvenir and postcard be returned to our classroom, along with the paper doll. As we receive our responses

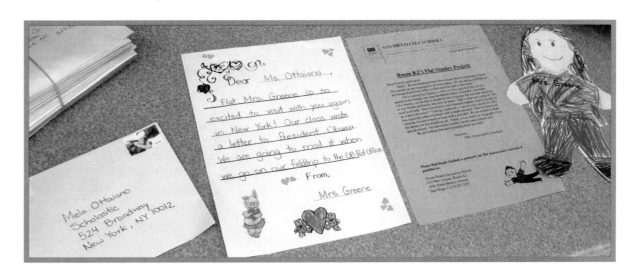

we post the flat student and postcard on our classroom map with yarn stretching from San Diego to wherever he or she has traveled. Students love this project and we reap the benefits for months to come. Through my experience I have found that this project hooks some students on letter writing.

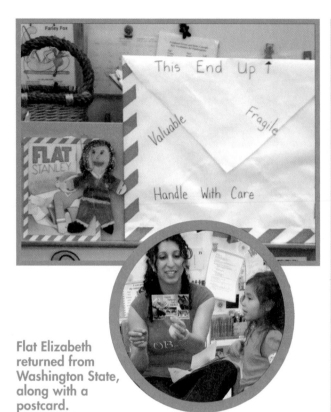

Flat Elizabeth returned from Washington State, along with a postcard.

On our trip to the Ocean Beach Post Office we learned the process of how mail is delivered.

Art, Music, Dance, and Theater

Volunteers come in the afternoon to work with students on weekly art projects during free choice centers. Our projects are always connected to our literature. I set up the project the day before the volunteers come and make sure they have all necessary materials. I hang a sample next to the project center so that volunteers have a clear picture of what they are working on with students.

ART PROJECT CENTER

Project-based art has proven to be a favorite of many students in my class. Often students do not want to miss school for fear they may miss out on our weekly art project.

Art projects are used in students' memory books, to create bulletin boards, and to decorate our classroom.

I had shelves made to fit my large and small construction paper. Paper is quickly accessible, and I can keep track of my inventory at a glance.

Sponge-painted Swimmy fish

SWIMMY

We learned when we work together we can do anything!

Math, Science, Art, and More

Mother's Day tulips

Handprint caterpillar

Mermaids

Flowers on the door

PAINTING Students paint at the easel once a week in the mornings during literacy centers. This activity is run by my art volunteers. Students learn how to use a paintbrush properly, learn about light and dark colors, gain spatial awareness, and, most important, learn how to listen and follow directions. Students paint characters and settings for murals to create literature-based art. They also have free painting days when they create their own artwork. The goal is for students to paint independently using the paints and brushes correctly. We display student work on a line next to the art easels. It stays on display until we need the space for the next project.

Painting cats with our volunteer, Mrs. Heft

Math, Science, Art, and More

A response-to-literature project, Mr. Seahorse, directed by our P.T.A.-sponsored art teacher, Lynn Greer

VISITING ART TEACHERS I am extremely fortunate to have a dear friend who is an artist. She volunteers in our classroom once a week and either does a whole-group directed drawing lesson with students or a painting demonstration. On weeks that we paint, students receive small-group support from her. The products are always amazing. Our school PTA also hires a local art teacher to provide literature-based art lessons in our classrooms. She teaches students directed drawing and incorporates many different art techniques. Students learn how lines (curved, slanted, straight, diagonal, spiral) and shapes are used to create form. There are many community college art classes where you can look for potential classroom volunteers.

MUSIC Music is an integral part of our day. I use songs for instruction, as signals to change activities, and during transitions. Music brings joy to the classroom while enriching language skills. I play classical music during literacy centers and writing time and find it makes a dramatic difference in maintaining quiet in the classroom. I recently added all my school music to an MP3 player and created playlists for each month. I also added playlists for subject areas such as alphabet, reading, math, science, and movement.

The drummer plays a pattern and the other students mimic it.

Using an Action Based Learning Mat helps students develop spacial awareness and improves their understanding of how letters are formed. Walking in "lazy eights" (Brain Gym terminology) helps students to establish the crossing of the midline. This is essential for effective handwriting and other visual motor skills. We use Brain Gym activities during transitions to help prepare students for learning.

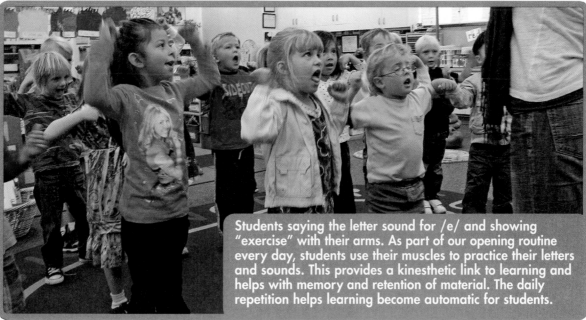

Students saying the letter sound for /e/ and showing "exercise" with their arms. As part of our opening routine every day, students use their muscles to practice their letters and sounds. This provides a kinesthetic link to learning and helps with memory and retention of material. The daily repetition helps learning become automatic for students.

DANCE/MOVEMENT Movement is a basic necessity for kindergarteners. Moving songs are perfect for transitions and when students' motors are running high. Here are ten moving songs I turn to again and again to help students get the wiggles out:

1. "Marching Around the Alphabet" – Hap Palmer
2. "Listen and Move" – Greg & Steve
3. "Growing" – Hap Palmer
4. "The Freeze" – Greg & Steve
5. "The Number Rock" – Greg & Steve
6. "Apples and Bananas" – Raffi
7. "Colors" – Hap Palmer
8. "Can a Cherry Pie Wave Goodbye?" – Hap Palmer
9. "Knees Up Mother Brown" – Raffi
10. "Alligators All Around" – Carole King

My favorite children's artists are Greg & Steve, Raffi, Hap Palmer, and Ella Jenkins.

Puppet show

PERFORMING ARTS We use puppets during storytelling and free choice. The puppet theater inspires creative thinking and oral language development. Students act out feelings, characters, and make up their own stories.

Each year my class performs a play, "The Little Red Hen." The students perform on stage for their family and friends. This play is a culmination of a month-long unit on Friendship in February. We begin by reading *The Little Red Hen*. Next, we analyze the story by creating a story map. Students learn about story elements and retelling. They go through the process of putting on a production: from auditions to rehearsals to practicing on stage. We focus on voice, body language, expression, and courage. Engagement is high because they know they will perform on stage for an audience. Each year, the play is a wonderful learning experience for my students. We end our final performance with a cast party to celebrate their accomplishments.

Putting together a performance incorporates all aspects of the curriculum and is a joyful experience for students and their families.

The Little Red Hen Cast

Molly

Emily, Sam, Destiny

J.K, Dominic, Jasmine, Cian

Nico, Katel, Elizabeth, Shane

Justin - Grace, Avery

Joseph, Vincent, Valerie, Brayden

Jackson, Torry, Kali, Brian

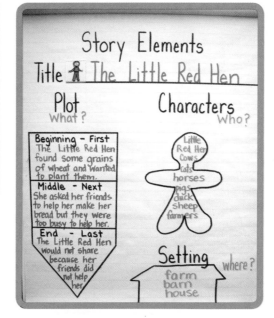

Story Elements

Title 👤 The Little Red Hen

Plot
What?

Characters
Who?

Beginning - First
The Little Red Hen found some grains of wheat and wanted to plant them.

Middle - Next
She asked her friends to help her make her bread but they were too busy to help her.

End - Last
The Little Red Hen would not share because her friends did not help her

Little Red Hen
Cows
Cats
horses
pigs
a duck
sheep
farmers

Setting   where?
farm
barn
house

Free Choice Activities

This 30-minute period at the end of the day serves as a reward for students who have completed the day's assignments and used self-control. Necessary make-up work, behavior conversations, and related notes students write to their parents, take place during choice time.

Kindergarteners love to make decisions about their own learning. Choice time offers students more opportunities to build social skills, such as sharing, negotiation, problem solving, and decision making. It inspires creative play, which is a building block for young children.

To help students succeed during this time, I explicitly teach the rules. For example:

- Four students per activity (except the writing center, which seats six)

- Take what you need out of activity tubs (no dumping)

- If you change activities, clean up what you used before changing areas

- Use quiet voices

If students misuse materials, the center is closed until we discuss proper care of the materials.

As the year progresses, I introduce new free choice activities that relate to the current unit of study.

FREE CHOICE FAVORITES

- Literacy centers
- Activity tubs
- Math tubs
- Puppets and puppet theater
- Play-Doh
- Climbing pole
- Science center
- Wooden or foam blocks
- Dinosaurs
- Grocery cart and cash register
- Fairy tale castle and puppets
- Barn and farm animals
- Games and puzzles
- Marble raceway

Bookshelf with free choice and literacy activities

Shane made it to the top of the climbing pole!

Choice time offers students the chance to be in charge of their learning, encouraging them to pursue their own interests and develop autonomy. Missing a portion of it is the perfect natural consequence for students who misbehave.

Rules

1. Use a quiet voice
2. 4 Students per activity
3. Clean up before changing activities
4. Share

CHAPTER 7

Home-School Connection

Family involvement is fundamental to a strong kindergarten program. When parents are involved, students are more eager to improve socially and academically. Parent volunteers support my classroom in numerous ways. For example, they run my Home Reading program, check in homework, prepare materials for projects, guide students through art activities, work in the garden, chaperone field trips, and act as community liaisons, contacting stores and businesses when we need something special. They also do projects at home and provide the resources we need for special activities and events. Parents are our biggest cheerleaders. Together we can do much more than I could ever accomplish alone.

Working With Families

VOLUNTEERS Having volunteers requires work, but the rewards are worth it. Students whose parents volunteer in the classroom tend to have increased attendance, better achievement, and fewer behavior problems. Volunteers who help in the classroom develop a true appreciation for teachers. I find my volunteers become my greatest advocates with other parents and administrators. The volunteers develop a better understanding of our curriculum and get to know the class.

Volunteer jobs include:

- Preparing materials for projects
- Sharing special talents and skills
- Daily home reading
- Homework helper
- Garden helper
- Field trip chaperones
- Easel painting and art projects
- Web site maintenance
- Coordinating class auction basket

Room _____ Volunteer Survey

Classroom volunteers are an important part of our teaching program. If you would like to help in our classroom this year please indicate your preferences and return this form by _____. Volunteers must fill out a volunteer packet and have a current TB test on file in the school office.

- ❑ Room Parent (coordinate class celebrations and P.T.A. events)
- ❑ Project Assistant (guide students through in-class activities)
- ❑ Home Reading Program Helper (student reads to volunteer 1:1)
- ❑ Homework Helper (check in homework and pack folders/envelopes)
- ❑ Web Page Assistant (add photographs)
- ❑ Memory Book Coordinator (This is a BIG job!—compile pages throughout the year)
- ❑ Garden Volunteer
- ❑ Field Trip Chaperone
- ❑ Community Liaison (deliver donation requests, thank-you letters, contact and help set up community outreach programs)
- ❑ Project preparation at home (tracing, cutting, stapling, book assembly)
- ❑ Share a special skill or talent: _____

Volunteer Name _____

Phone Number _____

Student's Name _____

Relationship to Student _____

A volunteer survey (see page 89) goes home on the first day of school. I gather information, speak to people, and then create a class volunteer schedule, assigning each volunteer a specific job, day, and time.

Our school holds a Volunteer Appreciation Luncheon at the end of the year. We created this banner for the event.

I want my volunteers to know I value the time, love, energy, and dedication they show to our class, so I look for opportunities throughout the year to thank them. These flowers were grown with our garden volunteers in our Kinder-garden.

Volunteer "thank you" bag with students' self-portraits drawn with crayons and adhered with iron-on transfer paper.

COMMUNICATION Communication with parents is the key to my lack of regular discipline problems. I make every effort through notes, phone calls, and quick comments to let parents know about the good things their child is doing at school. This helps build a home-school bond so that when trouble strikes I have immediate family support. When students know that their teacher and parents are working as a team, they are more likely to act in accordance with established rules of behavior.

Communication folders inside are labeled "Leave at Home" and "Return to School" to help ease management for both parents and teacher.

Home-School Connection

Students learn that when they return their weekly homework, they receive a sticker on the back of their homework envelope.

The benefits of this approach include access to appropriate text and individual support, outweighing the cost of losing a few books each year.

HOMEWORK I send a weekly homework packet from Friday to Friday so that working parents always have the weekend to catch up. The packet consists of a standard cover page (created by our grade-level team) where I write weekly notes and messages. Parents rely on this information to stay up to date with our busy kindergarten schedule. It also contains a reading log for parents to record five books they read aloud to their children. The packet contains sight word practice, handwriting, a phonics sheet, and district math. Every year, there are parents who want either more or less homework for their children. I let parents know they can buy workbooks if they want more. I encourage them to create a homework routine and break up the packet if they feel it is too much.

HOME READING PROGRAM My Home Reading program has contributed to my students' success in reading year after year by providing access to the types of books beginning readers need. The program is simple, with only two components: sight word practice and reading. Using the Dolch Word List, students move at their own rate to progress through 11 lists of 20 words each. As they master each list, I give them the next one. They move down our class rainbow chart toward a pot of gold. Not all students complete the rainbow, but several do. These advanced readers begin the rainbow again, this time having to spell the sight words correctly.

For the reading component, students select a book from our

classroom Independent Reading Library. They are guided to "just right books." These are books at their independent (not instructional) level. They take the book home and practice reading it several times with an adult. The adult then asks them a question from a comprehension strategy sheet and records the title on a reading log. When the student returns the envelope to school, he or she is given the opportunity to read the book and review his or her sight word list with a volunteer. They earn a sticker each time they return a book. Every ten stickers earn the student a trip to the prize box. Students turn in home reading at their own pace, but I highly recommend that parents make it a routine and set a goal to read a minimum of three times each week.

Mrs. Kurth, our Home Reading Volunteer, prompts Emily to use reading strategies when she is stuck on a word.

Special Events

KINDERGARTEN ORIENTATION Our school holds a kindergarten orientation on the Friday before school starts. Families meet in the auditorium for a brief introduction to the school and then students find out who their teacher is. Families come to the classroom for a brief talk about the first day of school. Parents fill out important after-school pickup information and dismissal authorization sheets. Students are less nervous because their initial apprehension has been soothed. Teachers get a sneak peak at what's to come.

Orientation information for parents in baskets

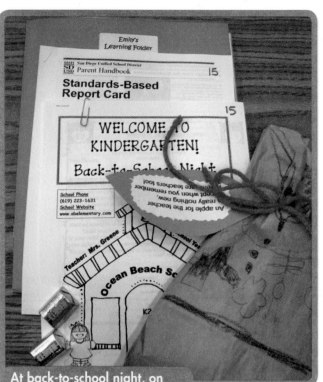

At back-to-school night, on each student's table, I have a bag for parents to take home, which includes a photo of their child on a large apple the student has cut out. On a leaf outside the bag is the poem, "An apple for the teacher is really nothing new, except when you remember, parents are teachers too!"

BACK-TO-SCHOOL NIGHT This is a curriculum night where parents learn about kindergarten expectations. I have found it very successful to create a PowerPoint presentation of our daily schedule, including photos of the children in action during their first weeks in kindergarten. I have a handout for parents, which includes curriculum information as well as a learning folder for students. The learning folder includes alphabet and name practice sheets, lined paper, a kindergarten pencil, a handwriting and phonics guide, and a sight word list. During this time, I also put out a sign-in and a sign-up sheet for parent-teacher conferences as well as a list of supplies needed.

Room _____ Supply List

There are many materials we use in kindergarten that are not provided by the school district. This is a list of supplies that support our classroom program. All contributions are greatly appreciated.

- Antibacterial hand soap and sanitizer
- Cleaning wipes or baby wipes
- Colored markers
- Washable markers
- Scented markers
- Double-sided tape
- Glue sticks
- Sidewalk chalk
- Bordered copy paper
- Clear plastic cups

- Paper plates, bowls, cups
- Printer labels
- Stickers (sets of 30)
- Photo paper (4 x 6)
- Color ink cartridges
- Blank CDs
- Bubbles
- Play-Doh
- Children's CDs (new or used)
- Resealable bags (quart, gallon, and jumbo)

- Prize Box items (small new or used toys)
- Large floor puzzles (new or used)

Items to recycle from home:
- Yogurt containers
- Bouquet wrappers
- Egg cartons
- Newspaper
- Men's button-down shirts (painting smocks)

Thank you for supporting our learning.

This supply list (see page 89) contains the items I use regularly in the classroom.

DONATIONS: Our PTA created an apple tree for each teacher. Teachers write the supplies they need on die-cut apples and then, if parents would like to donate, they select an apple from our "Giving Tree."

Celebrations

For class celebrations, I either put up a sign-up sheet on our Parent Message Board or send a flyer home. I organize celebrations and only ask for the specific supplies that are needed. This helps eliminate excess and keeps the event organized. Parent volunteers sign up for specific tasks. I always ask for supplies at least a day in advance so that I can make reminder phone calls or pick up missing items before the party.

November: Friendship Feast

October: Halloween Craft Party

WISHES FOR BABY New babies in the family are a familiar theme for kindergarteners. Our class celebrates the occasion by making a book for the new sibling, titled "Wishes for Baby." Students draw the baby's face and design a diaper. I take students' dictation and glue it to their page. I hole punch and put a ring at the top of each baby, creating a swinging baby book that is full of the kind of sentiments that only kindergarteners could think of.

Wishes for Baby

November 2008

Love,
K2 Students
Mrs. Greene & Mrs. Raya

It is very important to celebrate the major events that occur in the lives of my students' families. Celebrations help create happy bonds between myself, all the students, and their families.

A birthday celebration for our volunteer Mrs. Connelly, who has helped in Room K2 for the past nine years! The students and I like to celebrate everyone who is a part of our classroom.

BIRTHDAY All students deserve recognition on their birthday. Each student receives a birthday balloon and a crown. The balloon serves as a class card and the crown makes the student feel important. The class sings "Somebody's Birthday," a wonderful birthday song from Greg & Steve's CD *Holidays and Special Times*. The song prompts the birthday person to answer special questions and lends itself to hand gestures. I take a photo of the student for his or her parents. While sharing a birthday treat outside, we sing the traditional birthday song.

TEACHER TALK: Students are taught not to eat until everyone is served. Once the last treat is passed out, the class recites our eating chant together:

❝One, two, three, bite!❞

And then there is silence, for a moment.

TOOTH AWARD Simple store-bought awards or photocopied forms inform parents when this exciting event occurs. I purchase tiny tooth-shaped holders from the online site Really Good Stuff (see page 96) for students to use to transport their tooth home.

When students lose a tooth, they write their name on our giant tooth in our math calendar so that we can keep track of how many teeth are lost during the year.

Sharing Information

PARENT MESSAGE BOARD This easel is put just outside our classroom door on a daily basis. It contains the most current, up-to-date news and reminders about special events. It serves as a wonderful tool to help busy parents stay connected. I make sure to write about new sign-up sheets on my homework letter so that parents who visit the classroom less regularly are still informed. I offer to have them call or write me a note if they would like to sign up, but are not able to come to school.

A message board is a great place to post notices and sign-up sheets for conferences, celebrations, and field trips.

PARENT-TEACHER CONFERENCES

Conferences are an opportunity to develop a stronger partnership with parents. I always begin with a positive statement and then review the child's portfolio and report card and have all pertinent reference papers on hand. I use a simple conference note form to record any special information or tasks to follow up on with each child. Parents take home their child's report card along with a kindergarten skills information sheet, highlighting things to practice at home. During conferences I share much more than just academic performance. Other conversation with parents revolves around the student's citizenship, attitude, work habits, self-confidence, relationships with peers, playground behavior, tardiness, absences, health concerns, and general adjustment to kindergarten.

OUCH REPORT: "Owies" happen in kindergarten. The "Ouch Report" is a quick form that I created to notify parents of any minor injuries that occur at school.

Home-School Connection

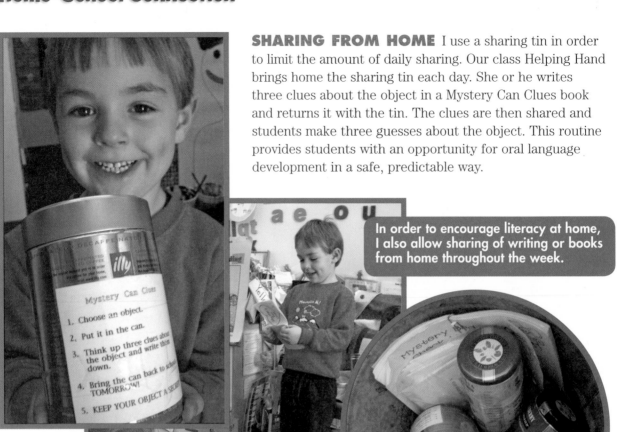

SHARING FROM HOME I use a sharing tin in order to limit the amount of daily sharing. Our class Helping Hand brings home the sharing tin each day. She or he writes three clues about the object in a Mystery Can Clues book and returns it with the tin. The clues are then shared and students make three guesses about the object. This routine provides students with an opportunity for oral language development in a safe, predictable way.

In order to encourage literacy at home, I also allow sharing of writing or books from home throughout the week.

On the first week of school, I always fill the "Extra Special Person" basket with special items that represent what I love, so that students get to know me a little better.

STUDENT OF THE WEEK At our school, teachers select a student of the week who is notified of their status at our Friday morning whole-school assembly. The student receives a ribbon and a coupon for a free ice pop or popcorn from the after-school treat sale each Friday. In the classroom, the student of the week receives the E.S.P.—or Extra Special Person—basket, which he or she returns on Monday filled with special sharing items. Students always look forward to this special opportunity to share, and the class gets to know more about each student one week at a time.

Room _____ Volunteer Survey

Classroom volunteers are an important part of our teaching program. If you would like to help in our classroom this year please indicate your preferences and return this form by _____.
Volunteers must fill out a volunteer packet and have a current TB test on file in the school office.

❑ Room Parent (coordinate class celebrations and P.T.A. events)

❑ Project Assistant (guide students through in-class activities)

❑ Home Reading Program Helper (student reads to volunteer 1:1)

❑ Homework Helper (check in homework and pack folders/envelopes)

❑ Web Page Assistant (add photographs)

❑ Memory Book Coordinator (This is a BIG job!— compile pages throughout the year)

❑ Garden Volunteer

❑ Field Trip Chaperone

❑ Community Liaison (deliver donation requests, thank-you letters, contact and help set up community outreach programs)

❑ Project preparation at home (tracing, cutting, stapling, book assembly)

❑ Share a special skill or talent: _____

_____

_____
Volunteer Name

_____
Student's Name

_____
Phone Number

_____
Relationship to Student

Room _____ Supply List

There are many materials we use in kindergarten that are not provided by the school district. This is a list of supplies that support our classroom program. All contributions are greatly appreciated.

❑ Antibacterial hand soap and sanitizer

❑ Cleaning wipes or baby wipes

❑ Colored markers

❑ Washable markers

❑ Scented markers

❑ Double-sided tape

❑ Glue sticks

❑ Sidewalk chalk

❑ Bordered copy paper

❑ Clear plastic cups

❑ Paper plates, bowls, cups

❑ Printer labels

❑ Stickers (sets of 30)

❑ Photo paper (4 x 6)

❑ Color ink cartridges

❑ Blank CDs

❑ Bubbles

❑ Play-Doh

❑ Children's CDs (new or used)

❑ Resealable bags (quart, gallon, and jumbo)

❑ Prize Box items (small new or used toys)

❑ Large floor puzzles (new or used)

Items to recycle from home:

❑ Yogurt containers

❑ Bouquet wrappers

❑ Egg cartons

❑ Newspaper

❑ Men's button-down shirts (painting smocks)

Thank you for supporting our learning.

CHAPTER 8

Assessment

Assessment is crucial to understanding student needs and teacher planning. I use information from my assessments to guide my curriculum. Do I need to re-teach a concept? Are students applying knowledge and showing me they are ready for next steps? Which students need to review concepts and who needs a challenge? Through reflection on both formal and informal assessments my questions are answered. I don't wait for formal parent conferences to share assessment information with parents. During informal conversations after school, or through quick notes, I let parents know where their children are succeeding and where they need continued practice.

Organizing Student Data

ASSESSMENT BINDERS These binders are divided with numbers 1 to 25 (see photo below, left) that correlate to the student number system. Using binders to contain this material provides me with a fast, easy, and efficient way to assess information and reassess students as needed. I transfer pertinent information to a note card that I keep near my chair. I use this information for purposeful questioning. This is a powerful teaching tool that you can use to help students meet their specific needs and individual

Basic Skills Assessment Binder

First day of school writing sample with student dictation: "It's about twirls." Samples like this one are housed in student portfolios (see next page).

learning goals. Remember to keep the information updated.

In one binder, I keep track of students' progress in basic skills, such as alphabet, phonics, numbers, and shape recognition. Students' reading assessments and running records are dated and kept together in another binder. Information on reading levels is posted in a pocket chart near the Home Reading station so that students know what level book is just right for them to select.

STUDENT PORTFOLIOS

Student portfolios include several file folders. The first is for general information. Monthly work samples for reading, writing, math, science, and social studies assessment are kept together for each grading period. These portfolios are used as evidence during parent-teacher conferences.

Running records are an easy way to find out which reading strategies students are using and what their next steps are.

Just before conferences, each student draws a self-portrait, which I use to create a construction paper folder to hold the student's work.

CHAPTER 9
Ending the Year

This is a bittersweet time for the students and me. We have worked hard all year to learn to work cooperatively and help each other grow. Now, it is time to move on to first grade (and, for me, a new lot of students to get to know and love). Change is our theme during this month because change is difficult for people. As a group we visit a first grade class and ask the students our burning questions: Is there a lot of writing? Do you have free choice? Is there a restroom in the classroom? My students get a lot out of this visit.

We mentor the incoming kindergarteners by writing a letter telling them about our class. I always read this letter on our first day of school.

I have a student-run Open House. Students are tour guides and show their families all the learning we have done.

Celebrations of Learning

OPEN HOUSE Open House is an opportunity for students to become tour guides and show parents around the room. The students and I create an interactive writing letter to parents welcoming them to our room. We also brainstorm a list of important things to share. I use this information to create a tour checklist, which students use during Open House.

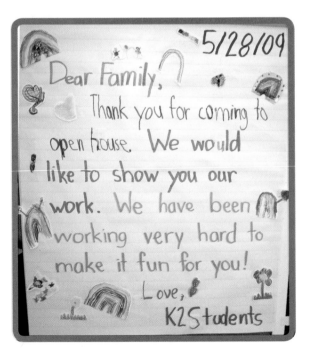

MEMORY BOOKS Every month, I save an art project, a writing sample, and a photograph for each student. My memory book volunteer compiles all this student work in each student's memory book (10 sheets of spiral-bound construction paper) at home during the year. At the end of the school year, the students and I invite parents to school in the morning for a memory book celebration. After students reminisce and review their memory book with their parents, we sing songs, and then I end by thanking my volunteers for their help during the year. We culminate our celebration with a potluck breakfast.

Memory Books on desks

Memory books are a culmination of a year's worth of learning and show growth over time. They include monthly art, writing, and photographs. Students and families treasure their memory books for years to come.

Gracie: September

Gracie: April

THE LAST DAY OF SCHOOL We call our last day of school "Kinder–Fun Day." We read the stories *When It's the Last Day of School* and *Oh, the Places You'll Go!*, write in autograph books, and share favorite memories. All the kindergarten classes at our school celebrate our last few hours of kindergarten together while listening to the Beach Boys. Parent volunteers run all the activities and are given leis to wear. We go outside for a rotation of events (10 minutes at each station):

- Obstacle course
- Sponge water relay
- Over-under relay
- Parachute games
- Hula hoops
- Bean bags
- Jumping balls
- Bubbles

We share ice pops, say our good-byes, and talk about our excitement for the summer months to come.

This is the day when younger siblings may join their big brother or sister at school. Often this gives them a taste of what they can look forward to when they go to kindergarten!

Getting Ready for Next Year

During the last week of school, I roll out butcher paper at the writing center and ask students to write and draw their favorite kindergarten memories on it. Before leaving for the summer, I put up the framework for my September bulletin board and then cover it with the students' end-of-the-year favorite memories. This paper protects it from fading and also serves as a colorful and informative display for our orientation the week before school starts. I am always glad to have my bulletin board ready when school starts, as this is always one of the busiest times of the year.

UNCLUTTER THE CLASSROOM At the end of the school year, I devote at least one day to weeding out materials and resources I no longer need. Often during the year, I oversave and I use this opportunity to remove any clutter, re-sort materials, and make math and science tubs accessible. I always appreciate having done this once the busy new school year begins.

> Getting rid of things is hard for most people, but the simple truth is it is easier to find and use what you have when it is a manageable amount.

Bulletin board covered with student memory butcher paper

Resources

CHILDREN'S LITERATURE

Anholt, C. and L. (1991). *All About You*. New York, NY: Scholastic Inc.

Boelts, M. (2005). *When It's the Last Day of School*. New York, NY: Scholastic Inc.

Brown, J. (2007). *Flat Stanley*. New York, NY: Scholastic Inc.

Charles, F. and Terry, M. (2000). *The Selfish Crocodile*. New York, NY: Scholastic Inc.

Christelow, E. (1989). *Five Little Monkeys Jumping on the Bed*. New York, NY: Scholastic Inc.

Gag, W. (2006). *Millions of Cats*. USA: Penguin Group.

Geisel, T. and A. (1990). *Oh, the Places You'll Go!* New York, NY: Random House.

Heritage Big Books. (1991). *The Little Red Hen*. USA: Jamestown Publishers, Inc.

Lionni, L. (1963). *Swimmy*. New York, NY: Scholastic Inc.

Martin, B. and Archambault, J. (1989). *Chicka Chicka Boom Boom*. New York, NY: Simon & Shuster Books for Young Readers.

Munsch, R. (1999). *We Share Everything!* Ontario, Canada: Scholastic Canada Ltd.

Penn, A. (1993). *The Kissing Hand*. New York, NY: Scholastic Inc.

Steiner, C. (1977). *The Original Warm Fuzzy Tale*. Torrance, CA: Jalmar Press.

Wells, R. (2000). *Max Cleans Up*. New York, NY: Scholastic Inc.

PROFESSIONAL LITERATURE

California School Garden Network. (2006). *Gardens for Learning: Creating and Sustaining Your School Garden*. Irvine, CA: California School Garden Network.

Cohen, Isabel and Goldsmith, Marcelle (2003). *Hands On: How to Use Brain Gym in the Classroom*. Ventura, CA: Edu-Kinesthetics, Inc.

Morris, Rick. (2000). *New Management Handbook*. San Diego, CA: New Management.

WEB SITES

BrainGym International: www.braingym.org (program information)

California School Garden Network: www.csgn.org (free resources, curriculum, and grants)

Dairy Council of California: www.dairycouncilofca.org/ (free nutritional education programs and resources)

DonorsChoose: www.DonorsChoose.org (grants)

Gold Star Registry: www.goldstarregistry.com (grants)

National Dairy Council: http://www.nationaldairycouncil.org (free nutritional education programs and resources)

Really Good Stuff: www.reallygoodstuff.com (general teaching resources)

Seussville: www.seussville.com (student activities based on Dr. Seuss books)

Target: www.freetech4teachers.com (field trips, arts education, and early childhood reading programs)